DON'T SWEAT THE SMALL STUFF FOR WOMEN

DON'T SWEAT THE SMALL STUFF FOR WOMEN

Simple and Practical Ways To Do
What Matters Most and Find Time For You

KRISTINE CARLSON

New York

Library of Congress Cataloging-in-Publication Data

Carlson, Kristine, 1963–
   Don't sweat the small stuff for women : simple and practical ways to do what matters most and find time for you / Kristine Carlson.—1st ed.
     p. cm.
   ISBN: 0-7868-8602-1
   1. Conduct of life. 2. Peace of mind. 3. Women—Psychology. I. Title.

   BF637.C5 C315 2001
   158.1'082—dc21

00-054488

FIRST EDITION

10 9 8 7

I dedicate this book to the three most important women in my life:
My mother, Patricia Anderson, who gave me the gift of life; and my daughters,
Jazzy and Kenna, who give me the incredible gift of their love.
It is a privilege being your Mom, and I love you just the way you are,
forever and for all time.

ACKNOWLEDGMENTS

I would especially like to thank Richard Carlson, my treasured husband, for his incredible inspiration and graciousness in giving me this opportunity to share. I'd like to thank my parents, Pat and Ted Anderson, for always loving me and giving me a wonderful childhood and great start in life. My editor, Leslie Wells, for her assistance, coaching, and encouragement. My parents-in-law, Don and Barbara Carlson, for all the support and enthusiasm they have given us over the years.

I've been richly blessed with great friendships. I'd like to thank all the special women in my life who gave me so much support and encouragement, and who helped inspire me simply by their presence. Beginning with those women I consider my "Life 101" mentors: Betty Norrie, Sheila Krystal, Michael Bailey, and my aunt Pauline Anderson. My cherished girlfriends who supported and encouraged me throughout this book: Kimberly Bottomley, Lisa Marino, Jane Carone, Cindy Driscoll, Melanie Edwards, Caroline Benard, Frances Evensen, Carole Stewart, Carol Simons, Christine Scharmer, Jeanine Stanley, Pamela Hayle-Mitchell, Marni Posl, Corry Wille, Heidi Mitchell-Springer, and Victoria Moran—and a special thanks to all the women in my life who are such an incredible inspiration and gift. I treasure you all!

CONTENTS

Foreword by Richard Carlson   xv

Introduction   1

1. Wish Wonder Woman Goodbye   5
2. Get Off to a Peaceful Start   9
3. Don't Get Over-Committee-d   12
4. Cut Your Friends Some Slack   14
5. Bust Your Boredom Blues   17
6. Stop Comparing Yourself to the Media Measuring Stick   20
7. Clarify with the Question: "Are You Asking for My Opinion, or Should I Just Listen?"   22
8. Make Peace with the Mundane   24
9. Get Down and Dirty   26
10. Don't Go There with the "Shoulda, Woulda, Coulda" Sisters   28
11. Save Your Pot-Stirring for Cooking Dinner   30
12. Speak from Your Love   32
13. Listen from Your Love   35
14. Look in the Mirror   37

15.	Go with the Twists and Turns	39
16.	Have a Bosom Buddy	41
17.	Create Memories for Your Children	43
18.	Be Reflective	45
19.	Stress-Busters	47
20.	Perhaps It's Not Personal	50
21.	Don't Let the Members of Your Family Dodge Your Draft	52
22.	Envy Not	54
23.	Find Your Gifts and Share Them	56
24.	Take Time for Your Self	59
25.	Let Out Your Steam Lightly	61
26.	Accept Compliments with "Thank You"	64
27.	Avoid Cyber-Rift!	66
28.	Protect Your Inner Flame	68
29.	Understand the Difference Between Intuition and Fear	71
30.	Set Clear Boundaries	74
31.	Let Go of Your "Perfect" Plans	77
32.	Don't Let Self-Doubt Stand in Your Way	80
33.	Give Yourself the Gift of Forgiveness	82
34.	Be Real	84
35.	P.S.—I'm PMS!	87
36.	Lower Your Threshold	89

37.	Let Your Children Grow Into Their Own Shoes	91
38.	Write a Letter and Find Out Where You Stand	94
39.	Gather and Let Go	96
40.	Stop Swimming Upstream	98
41.	Don't Be a Backseat Driver	100
42.	Create Beauty from the Inside Out	102
43.	My Way Is Not *the* Way—It's Just My Way	105
44.	Stop Magnifying the Flaws	107
45.	Celebrate Our Ability to Give Birth	109
46.	Learn to Meditate and Quiet Your Mind	111
47.	Go Ahead and Vent (One Time), but Get It Off Your Chest	113
48.	Set Your Own Priorities	115
49.	Don't Trip on Your Excess Baggage	118
50.	Packing Light and Traveling Right	121
51.	Get Off Your Hamster Wheel	125
52.	Use Your Career for Your Spiritual Work	128
53.	Know When Your Ego Is Getting the Best of You	131
54.	Stay Open to Meeting a New Friend	133
55.	Age Gracefully	135
56.	Consider That He May Not Have the "Eye" for It	138
57.	Go Inside for the Answers	141
58.	Dress from the Inside Out	144

59. Use Symbols to Remind You of Your Spirit 146

60. Remain Calm and Make the Best of a Bad Situation 148

61. Rise Above the Rut of Your Routine 150

62. Be Grateful for Small Things 152

63. Honor Your Mother 155

64. Celebrate Being Single! 157

65. Find Your Own Way 161

66. Allow Enthusiasm to Bubble Up from You 163

67. Share the "Nice" Stories 165

68. Say "No, but Thanks for Asking" (Without Feeling Guilty) 168

69. Give Yourself More Time Than You Think You'll Need 171

70. Go with the Girls 173

71. Don't Become Over-Identified in Any Role 175

72. Defuse the Thought Explosion! 178

73. When All Else Fails, Laugh 181

74. Plan an Inspiration Flow Day 183

75. Gripe to the One You've Got the Gripe with 185

76. Spice Up Your Sexy Side 189

77. Be 99 Percent Gossip-Free 193

78. Have a Backup Day Care Plan 195

79. Don't Weigh Every Day 198

80. Merge the Spiritual and Material Worlds 200

81. Know When to Turn Off Your Technology Booby Traps   204

82. Don't Let Your Anger Get the Best of You   207

83. Seize Your Opportunities   210

84. Widen Your Scope and Get Some Perspective   212

85. Renegotiate Your Boundaries   215

86. Don't Fight Fire with Fire—Unless It's a Controlled Burn   219

87. When Trying to Simplify, Think Prevention   221

88. Say the Words, "Hey, That's a Great Idea!" (and Then Act On It)   223

89. Don't Take It All So Seriously   226

90. Fancy Your Femininity   229

91. Know Your Hot Spots   231

92. Walk Through the Open Doors   234

93. Own Your Emotions   236

94. Remind Yourself What It Means to Be a Human "Being"   239

95. Find Your Compassion Corner   242

96. Remember That a Low Mood Is Only Temporary   245

97. Climb Your Mountains One Step at a Time   248

98. Define Your Small Stuff   250

99. Be Able to Stand on Your Own Two Feet   253

100. Treasure the Journey   256

      Author's Note   259

      Suggested Reading List   261

FOREWORD

It's a dream come true and a real honor to be sitting here today writing the foreword to Kris Carlson's book. Not only have Kris and I been married for more than fifteen years, but we're really close friends as well. We share a great deal of love, respect, and, more than anything else, laughter.

As you'll soon discover, Kris is a beautiful writer, but she's far more than that. She is a dedicated and loving mother and a friend to many. She is wise, compassionate, forgiving, and, for the most part, she doesn't sweat the small stuff. Really! In addition, she's more than willing to look at and address her own issues, and when she does get upset, it never lasts very long. Although she's an optimist, she is also a realist. She's aware of the problems most women face—but she's also very gifted at pointing toward legitimate solutions.

For many years, Kris and I have been reflecting upon and discussing the issues, solutions, and strategies in all of the *Don't Sweat the Small Stuff* books. We usually start our day with a short meditation together, followed by a heart-to-heart discussion of some kind. Kris is fun to talk to because, not only does she see the nature of many problems, but she's able to see the humor in most situations, as well. And while she's never once laughed at another person, she's almost always able to laugh at herself—a necessary ingredient in being an effective teacher of happiness.

There are some issues that only a woman can understand. I'm biased, of course, but I've never met a person more qualified to tackle the small stuff for women than Kris Carlson. In fact, the only time Kris ever says to me, "You just don't understand," it's always about an issue specifically about women! Having two daughters that I don't "always understand," I'm so glad that Kris is around to take charge!

I know you're going to love this book. It's filled with wisdom and good advice about a whole bunch of everyday stuff. Kris is able to get right to the heart of the matter in an honest, respectful, and light-hearted way. There's no wasted babble or filling of pages. What you'll read is good old common sense with a touch of flair and a lot of wisdom.

Many of my good friends are women, and I've met hundreds of women, over the years, from all over the world. I also grew up with a great mother and two wonderful sisters. And now I have two daughters. As I read this book, I saw all the women I know—and have known—in every page. The advice is applicable to all women—young and old, single, married, divorced, or widowed.

I often say, "We're all in this together." What I mean is that, as world citizens, we're all subject to the problems of being human—none of us are exempt. Yet, there's no question that women are absolutely different from men—different issues, problems, concerns, tendencies, and priorities. And while I'll never know exactly what it's like to be a woman, I do realize that every woman I know could benefit from this book in some way.

My greatest hope is that all people—men and women—will learn to live happier, more peaceful lives. If you're a woman, this book will help point you in that direction. It's a great read, and a fun way to learn to stop sweating the small stuff.

Treasure Yourself,
Richard Carlson
Benicia, CA
October, 2000

DON'T SWEAT THE SMALL STUFF FOR WOMEN

INTRODUCTION

For the most part, women have never had it so good. Thanks to our mothers, grandmothers, and great-grandmothers, we've achieved equality with men (even if some men don't think so). We've made incredible strides in white- and blue-collar professional arenas, and we have broken strict gender barriers in nearly all industries. More than ever, we're respected by others and we respect ourselves. And we deserve it! We have more independence, options, and conveniences than ever, as well as the capacity to live rich, full lives.

Along with the many options we have created for ourselves, however, comes some very real confusion accompanied by a sense of being overwhelmed. Unlike the women who came in generations before us, we are lacking a concrete paradigm to live by. Instead, we are expected to do it all—all the time. We have taken our ability to multi-task, and to accomplish a tremendous amount, to new levels. We are "super women" with much to celebrate—yet we are exhausted!

One thing that *hasn't* changed very much is that many of us have a tendency to sweat the small stuff! Women are incredibly strong and, ironically, we do really well when the stakes are high. If there's a crisis, we're on top of it. If a friend is in need, we'll be there. If there's a sick child, turn to a woman for strength. If a sacrifice needs to be made, chances are, we will rise to the occasion and find a way to do what needs to be done.

On the other hand, we're the first to "lose it" over fairly small stuff! We can be nitpicky, petty, uptight, and tense. Many of us are perfectionists, overly controlling, and easily offended. We take things personally, and can be very reactive and dramatic. We're often quick to get bothered, irritated, and frustrated.

I had a great experience as Richard's co-author for *Don't Sweat the Small Stuff in Love*. I have to admit, however, that when Richard asked me to write solo for the first time for this book, a part of me wanted to hightail it as fast as I could in the other direction! However, I knew, after some contemplation, that this would be a challenge and a part of my own spiritual journey that I simply could not refuse. It gave me a chance to reflect upon and put into words those things that I had been attempting to practice for a lifetime.

I'd like you to know that the advice in this book is not coming from a woman who has any sort of superiority complex or any illusion that she has it all together. Far from it: I'm a normal everyday person who has either dealt with, or is currently dealing with, most of the issues and challenges in this book. To one degree or another, most of us have struggled with body image, family choices, budgets, men, friends, lifestyle, time management, communication issues, parenting, and balance. I certainly have. This is the stuff life is made of, and from which none of us are exempt!

I suppose that my greatest asset is that, like Richard, I'm a genuinely happy person most of the time. I tend to see the glass half full instead of half empty. I've always felt grateful to be a woman and to be alive. Happiness and peace of mind have always been a priority. Because of my basic nature and the efforts I've taken in this direction, I've come to see that it's not necessary (most of the time) to sweat the small stuff. My goal in writing this book is to point you in that general direction. I've found that the less bothered I become, the more I'm able to celebrate being female.

Like so many other women, I find all sorts of reasons (albeit some very superficial, but enjoyable nonetheless) to relish being a woman. I love T-shirts with a bit of lace, French country prints, and cinnamon-spice scents. I love taking aromatherapy baths and playing with makeup. To me, there is nothing greater than being "mommy," and I adore doing my girls' hair and nails. I also love being Richard's wife. I cherish my girlfriends and the sensitivity, understanding, and compassion we offer each other day-to-day. I love expressing myself passionately through art, creating a haven out of my home, exercising, practicing yoga, and med-itation—and I admit, I also love to shop!

On the other hand, I have also experienced, firsthand, the many chal-lenges, circumstances, and issues facing women today; everything from being a full-time business owner to part-time career woman blended with motherhood. I've also been a full-time mother and home manager. I've been successful at some things, and less successful at others. There was a long time when we struggled to make ends meet financially. I've been single, and I've been married. And of course there was a time, although I sometimes have difficulty remembering those years, when I was a strug-gling teen and college student.

This is a book for busy women who want to get the most out of life while merging their spiritual and material worlds, and without sacrificing what they are able to give others. By implementing these strategies, your life won't be perfect, but there's no question that you will receive more joy and find all you do more manageable. I've created strategies that are easy to implement, yet packed with a punch. Each one is designed to show you a way to value yourself more fully, connect with your spirit, give yourself more time, inspire new perspective, or help you to let go of the little things that bother you. In short, these strategies give you more options. They allow you to become slightly less reactive—so that you can become more responsive and reflective. It's my personal belief that women are incredibly wise and resilient. And by making shifts and adjustments, however small, we're able to bring that wisdom to the surface.

No matter what part of your journey you are on, I invite you to join me through the upcoming pages. I am excited and honored to share perspectives of the *Don't Sweat* philosophy which are specific to us as women. I know in my heart that each of us is gifted with great potential—for wisdom, creativity, love, kindness, compassion, strength, and tenderness. I wish for you a lifetime filled with these qualities and any others that are important to you. Good luck!

1

WISH WONDER WOMAN GOODBYE

I saw a bumper sticker that said: "I am Woman. I am invincible. I am tired." Girlfriend, doesn't that say it all? Where do we women get the idea that we have to be perfect and do everything with the gusto and grace of Wonder Woman? There's no harm in giving everything you do the best you have to offer, but when your expectations are too high and your head hurts or your hair feels as though it could fall out, you need to consider wishing the Wonder Woman in you goodbye.

The key to this strategy is threefold. One, let go of the notion that you can do it all. When you can't accomplish everything on your list, that doesn't mean you're inadequate. Two, be willing to ask for help when you need it. Three, be willing to make changes when your system fails. If you can do these three things, you have begun to say goodbye to Wonder Woman!

I remember thinking that I would be the kind of woman who could easily balance motherhood, career, and outside interests, as well as have a perfect marriage. I did a pretty good job until our second daughter, our lovely Kenna, came along. Then my system failed and became out of balance. Kenna was one of the sweetest babies ever created. She was, however, an ear infection infant, and ran high fevers often. Dosed with antibiotics, she was sick a great deal of the time. Day care was out of the question; I wouldn't dream of having someone else care for my sick child. But Richard and I were running out of answers.

Finally, a solution came to me one stressed-out morning. As I finally quieted down, I realized that I was trying to maintain an image that was now totally out of control, and that was bigger than I had energy for or that I ever imagined it would be. It was as if a lightbulb went on; it became obvious that it was time to wish Wonder Woman goodbye—and that's exactly what I did!

I began to think it was time for my first career change; I was going to go from graphic designer to home manager. Although it wasn't the best of times financially, we decided that our family would be better served if I took a leave of absence from my business. I knew that this was probaby going to close a chapter in my personal history, and it wasn't going to be easy, as change rarely is. However, I decided that I needed to prioritize my family's needs (and sanity) over my own need to hold on to the "Wonder Woman" who thought she could handle running a business during nap times. It was just too much!

After the initial adjustment, I figured out that taking care of our two daughters full-time was a lot of fun, even if it meant less money—and it was so much more gratifying without the frustration of having a work schedule to attend to.

Stress is a very real phenomenon, but consider how much of it you create for yourself. If your husband's income alone is not enough to adequately provide for your family, then your only choice may be to go to work. On the other hand, if your husband's income is ample, yet you choose to work, and you're constantly stressed-out and made miserable by your job—well, in my book, that's a different story.

It might sound as if I'm making the case that all mothers should stay home with their children instead of working. I'm not. All I'm saying is that all of us need to take a look at our lives as circumstances change, and reflect on our priorities. As big events occur—bringing babies home from the hospital, having ill parents, or tending a sick child, for instance—we can't just expect our lives to go on as usual. We need to evaluate whether or not our current lifestyle best serves us, and if not, to navigate our way in a new direction by making small shifts and adjustments. Being stressed-out to the max virtually all the time is not giving your family the best you have to offer, because there's no way the material things you provide will replace your sanity, and that of your family.

If, on the other hand, you can create some flexibililty in your work schedule when needed, and you have excellent help, and all the family members are thriving, good for you—you've found a balance that works.

Keep in mind that Wonder Woman thinks she can do everything and be all things to everyone, all at once! She never says, "No, but thanks for asking," when asked to volunteer her time. She can't set limits, and she continues to add more and more to her calendar without letting go of anything. She darts here and there, leaving a frenetic trail of busyness. She adds one more committee to her list, or one more pet. She never says no to a lunch date or social request—unless, of course, she's already booked. She always takes in houseguests. Does she have a family? Well, if not, you can bet she plans on squeezing one into her schedule! Whatever her reasons, she does too much and eventually she caves in from exhaustion!

If this sounds familiar, it's time to reevaluate your "Wonder Woman" image and self-imposed expectations. Whether you're a stay-at-home, full-time mom or corporate executive; single, married with children, or otherwise; you need to ask yourself some basic questions. Would you enjoy your children more and have more to offer them emotionally if you took an occasional break? Are you spending too much time away from them in the name of good works? Is your home-based business totally taking over your life? How much of you does the company you work for really own, and how much are you willing to give up to continue to climb the corporate ladder?

The point is, if you're stressed, working too hard, and completely out of steam, consider what things you have control over and make some changes. Most important, realize that you don't have to be perfect—and that Wonder Woman is merely a figment of someone else's imagination.

2

GET OFF TO A PEACEFUL START

Few would disagree that, in today's world, life is complex, busy, and, at times, stressful. However, depending on how you choose to start your day, you can greatly reduce your feelings of stress—almost regardless of what your circumstances may be.

Compare these two scenarios: In the first instance, you jump out of bed, pound down a cup of coffee, and launch into your "to do" list. You fill your head with plans, concerns, and worries. You mentally review all that you have to do. You think about yesterday's arguments, disappointments, and conflicts. You anticipate the upcoming problems of today. You turn on the radio, plug into the Internet, turn on the television, or open the newspaper to see what's going on in the world. What you'll find, of course, is plenty of bad news. In a matter of minutes, you've reinforced the stress you were already feeling.

You rush around, picking up and preparing for the day. If you have kids, you start the endless process. You find yourself hurried, agitated, and a bit short-tempered. You study your calendar or day-planner to see what's in store for today. The first half hour of your morning is seen as "preparation." However, what you've done, in reality, is prepare yourself for yet another stressful experience.

Scenario number two is quite different. You get out of bed earlier than usual, and begin your day with a genuine smile. You sit on the floor and do some gentle stretching. As your body warms up and begins to feel good, you close your eyes and spend a few minutes in quiet meditation. Your breathing is deep and calm. Your mind is clear.

As you open your eyes, you feel a sense of peace, the feeling that everything is going to be okay. You feel connected, secure, and confident. After a few more deep breaths, you think about two or three things that you have to be grateful for. You don't make a big deal out of it, but simply remind yourself what a gift it is to be alive.

Next to you is a pile of spiritual, uplifting, and inspirational books. You open one and read for as little as five minutes. You might choose a beautiful book of poetry, the Bible, something from the Buddhist perspective, or some writing from one of your favorite authors. It's totally up to you.

After a few short minutes of reading, you feel alive and ready for your day. You are enthused yet non-rushed, two of the characteristics of peak performance.

As dramatically different as these two modes of living are, we have the absolute power most of the time to choose one over the other. And while scenario number one, the frantic choice, is by far the most popular and seductive, scenario number two is much more peaceful.

It's easy to create your own morning ritual to enhance rather than disrupt the rest of your day. In most instances, early in the morning is an ideal time to do things like prayer, meditation, yoga, and spiritual reading. The kids are probably asleep, the phone isn't ringing, and the demands aren't being fired at you yet. And what's great is that you can set up this special time any way you wish. You can include your morning coffee or tea, candles, incense, music, and anything else you might find enjoyable or helpful. Once you've established this type of peaceful ritual, no matter how you set it up, you're going to wonder how you ever lived without it.

The argument against the more peaceful option is, as you'd expect, "a lack of time." But when you really think about it, that's a pretty lame excuse. Even if I had to drag myself out of bed twenty minutes earlier, I'd much rather begin my day in a peaceful, non-rushed manner as opposed to getting off to such a stressful start. The payoff is simply too big to ignore.

The problem is, if you get off to a hectic, "charge and go" beginning, this mentality will remain with you throughout your entire day. Once you're in that frenetic mind frame, it's very difficult to get out of it. Luckily, however, the reverse is also true. If you get off to a more peaceful start, you'll tend to carry that sense of peace with you in whatever you do.

It's helpful to remind yourself of how resilient and creative you are when you're calm and collected. Rather than reacting to life, you become more responsive. So, in a very real way, the twenty or thirty minutes you spend setting up and preparing for a peaceful day will save you far more time than it will take. In other words, you don't really have time *not* to do so. You'll make fewer mistakes, engage in fewer conflicts, see things more clearly, and have a very sharp learning curve. Your thinking will be wise, creative, and on-target.

I hope you'll explore this idea, as I'm confident it will make an enormous difference in your experience of daily living. I can only imagine what this world would be like if all women started their days in a more peaceful manner. We certainly deserve it!

3

DON'T GET OVER-COMMITTEE-D

I'll bet you know a few women like this (you might even be one). These women go to every PTA meeting, becoming an officer the very first chance they get. They are the ultimate "soccer moms." They organize every fundraiser and bake sale that comes along; they volunteer to help at every school event, to be homeroom mother, for community cleanups, and church or temple committees. If these women work outside the home, they're likely to have the same tendencies at work—they serve on boards and participate on every committee possible. It goes on in every aspect of their lives.

At times it's tempting to be over-committee-d. There's the camaraderie of being in a group of like-minded people; it can be a lot of fun to work together for a common goal. And it's nice to be of help and to feel needed. There's certainly nothing wrong with volunteering to do good works; in fact, I believe that everyone needs to contribute what they can. It's important to stay involved in your kids' lives, whether it be to help raise money for the school's new gym, or to act as a chaperone for your daughter's Girl Scouts camping trip.

However, if you find yourself desperately racing around all day, rushing from one event to another—hurrying your kids through dinner so you can make your 7:00 meeting at the community center, rushing them through breakfast so you can do that 5K run for the animal shelter, constantly on the go with committees, fundraisers, and such—you've probably taken on too much and are experiencing the over-committee-d backlash.

When you think about it, your kids don't really benefit from having an over-committee-d mom. It's no fun for them if you're gone most weeknights to some meeting or other. And taking them to soccer matches is one thing, but being the coach as well as organizing most of the other activities your children may participate in can be too time-consuming.

Here's something to consider: Volunteer your time wisely, and make sure that what you do doesn't interfere with the time you spend with your own kids. If you select just one or two things to do, and make sure that you truly do enjoy those things you decide to be involved in, the work will be that much more meaningful. Remember that being a mom is like being on a full-time committee anyway! You'll be much more stress-free if you aren't constantly hurrying to a committee meeting, and your children will appreciate the extra time you have to be available just for them.

4

CUT YOUR FRIENDS SOME SLACK

Aren't there days when you just want to say what's on your mind without anyone questioning you? Or misquote a fact and not be corrected? Perhaps you're not feeling well, and the last thing you want from a good friend is for her to take your mood personally or attempt to talk you out of the way you're feeling. Wouldn't it be nice if you could make a mistake, or say the wrong thing, or mess up, or be too critical, and have your friends just let it slide? It sure would be nice if we could count on our friends to cut us some slack, from time to time, and we should surely do the same for them.

Suppose your friend calls you, and you can tell by her tone of voice that she's having a bad day. Maybe she's on the verge of tears, or maybe she's just stressed out. As much as you want to say it, this is clearly not the time to remind her to "not be late" (as she was the last two times) on her carpool turn to pick up the kids for soccer. Neither is it the time to be critical of her, question her, or to stir things up in some way. Now's not the time to bring up an issue, suggest she's seeing things wrong, or make any concrete suggestions. It's certainly not a good idea to launch into your own story of misery, or to complain about your life.

Instead, this is a day to cut her some slack. Let her be human. Give her a break. Even if her low mood encourages her to say something you don't like—so what, just let it go! In fact, if you are a really good friend, you might even consider changing your schedule around and driving for her that afternoon. It might be just the right breathing room she needs to get her bearings back. If you can be this kind of friend, you'll be loved forever!

Friendships, especially with your girlfriends, are to be cherished. Who is it who helps you out with the kids when you've got the flu and your husband has to be at work? Who is it you turn to when you're feeling low and you need a shoulder to lean on or cry on? Who is it that picks you up when your marriage fails or some catastrophe happens? These are some of the reasons to cut your friends some slack, and not hold them to impossible expectations and standards, especially when they are having a bad day.

Sometimes, we get so close to our friends that it's easy to forget that they are just human—like we are. They're going to get in low moods, make mistakes, say the wrong thing, be overly critical, use poor judgment, disagree with some of your opinions, and so forth. Everyone, even our friends, can be insensitive at times, quick-tempered, in need of space, or feel like they're going crazy! The best friends in the world are those who remember this—those who accept this—those who love their friends in spite of it all. The best friends are those who cut their friends some slack, those who make allowances for their friends' imperfections.

Most of all, remember that if you have a live-in housemate, husband, boyfriend, or life partner, don't forget that they are your "best friends," and go ahead and cut them some slack too! Often the people we live with don't get the best of us, but instead the worst! Cutting each other some slack will do wonders to your long-range happiness as a couple.

15

In the long run, cutting your friends some slack will greatly reduce your own stress. You'll feel good about yourself, knowing that you allow people to be fully human, even though they are far from perfect. You'll also be loved, cherished, and appreciated for being willing to love your friends just the way they are.

5

BUST YOUR BOREDOM BLUES

There are times in life when we simply trade one compulsion for another because of the inner restlessness we associate with boredom. We attempt to fill up this feeling of emptiness by distracting ourselves with any number of insatiable activities. You may try to find satisfaction through having one sexual partner, or many. Your feelings of emptiness and restlessness may lead you to turn to compulsive shopping or cleaning, working, food, alcohol or drug abuse.

To heal, it's necessary to recognize that boredom is a learned response, and a form of anxiety which stems from our thinking—too much thinking, to be specific. Our minds are so busy and "filled up," that we become restless when there isn't something "exciting" going on or something exciting we can look forward to.

The good news is that anything we have the ability to learn, we can also unlearn. As you begin to see that boredom is nothing more than a state of mind that you have bought into, and become accustomed to, you can use it as a barometer to bring your attention back to the present. In other words, when you're feeling bored, instead of panicking and scrambling to fill the feelings with an activity, you can use the feelings as an opportunity to let go and relax.

I've observed that our natural tendency is to immediately distract ourselves from our doldrums or any feelings of boredom. As an experiment, I confided in a few people that I was feeling restless. I wanted to see what kind of advice I would receive. In fact, I was not at all surprised by the advice I heard. One person said I should spend more time shopping. Another advised me to get involved in a home fix-it project. I was told that perhaps I needed to have another child, or volunteer more of my time at school.

Not surprisingly, most people will immediately search out more activity and stimulus, in order to avoid at all costs the anxiety we associate with boredom. Not one person said, "It's okay to be bored, just sit with it for awhile." In fact, it made the people I asked nervous, simply to hear about "my boredom"!

If you step back for a minute, it's interesting to examine how virtually everyone is complaining of having too much to do and not enough time, yet their solution to restlessness is to find even more to do! It's like an ongoing vicious circle with no end in sight.

As an experiment, the next time you feel bored or restless, try something a little different. Rather than immediately looking for a means of distraction, sit with it for awhile. Notice what kinds of thoughts you are having, and bring your attention back to the moment.

When you are bored, your attention tends to be focused on the past or the future—what's missing or what could be better. As you experience bringing your attention back to the present, you begin to understand that in this moment, and this moment only, there is life. Real life is right here—right now. Boredom, on the other hand, is nothing more than a man-made notion, stemming from our habit of being addicted to excitement and activity. It's our mind playing tricks on us—trying to convince us that life would be so much better and more fulfilling if only something else were happening.

Without realizing it, we have taught our children to be bored by filling up every minute with rushed activities, too much stimulus, non-stop entertainment, and school. Kids get so used to the "what's next" mentality that they become bored if there isn't something "exciting" going on, or something they are looking forward to doing. Our schools are pushing our children into harder and more complicated concepts, earlier and earlier. This "rush to succeed" mentality even has some parents enrolling toddlers in college preparatory preschools! There's no time for kids to be kids anymore. Instead, we have collectively decided that the achievement race is far more important. The fear is that our children will not be able to compete later in life. Indeed, we've convinced ourselves that "someday," their lives are going to be great.

I look at this issue quite differently. I believe we need to show our children the importance of living in the moment—in the here and now—so that they have a chance to enjoy everyday life. By giving them the gift of being able to entertain themselves, we help them prepare to be mature teens and adults who are not thrill-seekers and excitement junkies.

By busting your boredom blues, your children will learn from your example. When you're not freaked out by boredom, you'll realize that you've temporarily slipped into the past or future, and you can bring your attention back to the present moment. You will feel peace in knowing that, in this moment, life is already great. There's nothing you have to do to make it any better.

6

STOP COMPARING YOURSELF TO THE MEDIA MEASURING STICK

If you haven't done so already, it's time for you to step up to the plate and celebrate your own uniqueness as a woman. When we are unhappy with ourselves, it is usually because we are preoccupied with comparing ourselves to others. One of the major culprits in exacerbating this tendency is the media, which gives us high, if not impossible, standards to live up to.

When you are feeling low about how you look, it's important to put those magazines aside, and practice looking in the mirror and focusing on all that you have to be grateful for. We need to remember that the models and actresses whose looks we covet are merely people too. Sure, they obviously have incredible physical attributes which make them our standard for "beautiful." However, much of what you see is the air-brushed, computerized version of what appears to be a real person. That doesn't take into consideration their many "tools of the trade," which include breast implants, tummy tucks, and liposuction.

Many of these models of physical perfection use such desperate measures to mold their bodies. How can a normal woman who lives on a budget and has barely enough time to put on makeup in the morning— much less exercise—live up to these expectations? And who'd want to be chopped up and stitched back together to fit someone else's ideal of beauty, anyway? The truth is plain and simple: we can't.

Stop comparing yourself to the made-up fantasy images presented by the media; instead, be the best that you can be, given the attributes that you have. Take good care of yourself, and you will look as beautiful as you feel, especially if you look in the mirror and focus your attention in the right direction. Dare to look in the mirror and notice those parts of you that are undeniably female and attractive; celebrate your curves and your limbs that are unique only to you in their size and shape. In the end, a woman with true self-confidence is the most attractive woman in a room, because her beauty comes from feeling good about herself from the inside.

7

CLARIFY WITH THE QUESTION: "ARE YOU ASKING FOR MY OPINION, OR SHOULD I JUST LISTEN?"

There are many times I forget to ask my friends, husband, or daughters: "Are you asking for my opinion, or would you like it if I just listen?" I've always thought that it isn't difficult to give advice, but taking it is a different matter altogether. Taking advice or even listening to it when that's not what you really want is nearly impossible. Usually when advice is offered (when unasked for), it is ignored, if not resented, because all the person really wants is to be heard.

Listening to someone you care for is one of the simplest ways to show that person that you care. Not feeling listened to is one of the major complaints people have about all of their relationships, especially those people we live with. Many times we are just in need of some healthy venting, compassion, and understanding. What we don't want is a solution. How presumptuous of us to think that we have the solution to someone else's problem, anyway!

Asking this simple question prior to spouting off your advice will enhance and clarify your communication with others. You will find that many times, your friend or partner or child *will* want your opinion. The act of asking the question will remind them that they have, in fact, asked for advice, and will encourage them to listen carefully. Your job, of course, is then to tune in and give them the most constructive advice possible. Reflect on what would be in their very best interest. Ideally, you will be in a neutral, open state of mind where what you say will trigger some insight or wisdom in the other person. This is the role of the counselor—to help someone else figure out the answer and design a plan of action for a problem or question.

For instance, your teenage daughter might share with you a problem that she has with one of her friends at school. She may just want your sympathy, but you jump in with advice on what to say to the friend and how to treat her the next time the incident occurs. She immediately bristles and tunes you out. If, instead of jumping in with your advice, you had begun (in a loving, non-lecturing tone of voice) with the question, "I'm here for you. Would you like me just to listen, or do you want an opinion?", the difficulty might have been avoided. As you experiment with this approach, your child will appreciate your taking her feelings into consideration, and in the end she may wind up asking for your advice much more often. But when she doesn't want advice, you'll be helping her anyway—just by being there as a good listener. In those instances, that's all she needs and all she wants. You, too, will benefit, because you won't have to feel frustrated by the fact that she's not taking your advice.

There are certainly times where our opinions and advice are wanted and needed. There are other times, however, when being a good listener is exactly what someone needs. One of the ways to determine which is called for in a given situation is to simply ask the question, "Do you want my advice—or would you like me to just listen?" I hope you find this strategy as helpful as I have in all your important relationships.

8

MAKE PEACE WITH THE MUNDANE

Let's face it: Much of life is mundane. Life is made up of thousands of daily "small stuff" tasks and chores that come and go like the tides of time; just when you think you've got it all organized and picked up, the day begins again and you are back where you started.

Part of my daily ritual is to spend an hour every morning picking up the piles that have been left behind in everyone's haste to get out the door. Over the years, I have learned to actually enjoy this time in my routine and think of it as clearing the path of my day. I have surrendered to the fact that while these tasks are mundane, they give me an opportunity to meditate in my own way while doing the ordinary. It is important for me to keep order in our home; I find it easier to keep order inside of me when things are neat on the outside.

I met an older gentleman at a laundromat one day. He was finishing his laundry and smiling in quiet contemplation. I couldn't help but strike up a conversation, as I found it fascinating to see such a distinguished man doing his laundry, much less enjoying it. I commented to him about how nice it was to see him smiling while folding his clothes. He responded by telling me, "You know, I find folding clothes a sort of Zen meditation. I find great comfort in the ordinary and mindless task; it helped to keep me sane during some rough times I had in the military." There you go—a new perspective on laundry!

The next time you feel overwhelmed by the repetitive nature of keeping your household in order, see if you can find some comfort in doing the ordinary. If you can see it as clearing your path for the day, you will make peace with the mundane, and that will be one less mental battle to fight.

9

GET DOWN AND DIRTY

I knew the title of this strategy was going to get you! (Okay, now, get your mind out of the gutter, I had a more literal meaning in mind.) Let go of your clean-cut, prim and proper self and get down and dirty, really dirty, once in awhile; it will do you good! Dig in the garden without gloves, go on a run in the rain and splash in every mud puddle you see, or go on a hike and feel the wind in your hair.

I try to get down and dirty almost daily. Either on my early morning run or pulling weeds in the garden or brushing my horse and riding, I get plenty of dirt under my nails. After all, in every girl there's a little bit of boy, and it reminds us to live carefree for a few of our moments each day, like we did when we were kids. We didn't worry about putting on makeup or wearing gloves to protect our hands, we just played!

Getting down and dirty reminds us to enjoy ourselves and to ground our energy in nature. It's incredibly nurturing to spend as much time as you can outdoors. That's why gardening is so gratifying. Every fall I plant bulbs, and in the summer I grow sunflowers. I don't wear gloves, so I can feel the dirt. I look forward to the entire process of picking the bulbs out at my local nursery, gathering the supplies I need, digging each hole, and finally watching the flowers bloom in springtime and summer. Each variety holds special memories, since I started this ritual while my girls were toddlers. I remember the large yellow daffodils and paperwhite narcissi I planted with Jazzy when she was two, three and four years old in the planter box. I can still see Kenna digging the perfect hole for the variety that grow along the pathway leading to our front door.

After my daughters' first slumber party, I surprised the girls at breakfast by constantly missing their strawberry waffles with the whipped cream and squirting their noses and faces instead. They were, of course, delighted, and a bit surprised at the mess I was creating. I looked at it this way: after being kept up most of the night with their talking, I was entitled to a bit of fun! (I nailed the ones who were up the latest.)

Kids have few qualms about getting dirty, and neither should we. Enjoy yourself in nature, and nurture your spirit with a little dirt now and then. Remember that you can always wash it off, and clean never felt so good!

10

DON'T GO THERE WITH THE "SHOULDA, WOULDA, COULDA" SISTERS

This strategy serves as one more reminder to focus our attention on the present moment. It encourages us to take a look at a mental dynamic that is nothing more than a habit of regret. Richard and I once heard someone tell a story about how the "Shoulda, Woulda, Coulda" sisters can grab you before you know it. You become more focused on what might have been rather than on what is, therefore missing out on gratitude for the present moment.

No matter what she has just experienced, sister Shoulda makes a habit of commenting on how she should have done something differently. Just the other day, her sister Coulda complimented her on the dress she was wearing. Coulda told Shoulda what a lovely color of blue it was. Shoulda always responds in the same way: "Oh yes, it is lovely, but I really should have picked the lavender one or the fuschia one." She then dwells on that notion for some time. Now Woulda gets involved, and agrees with her, saying: "Oh yes, dear, you really would have done better with the lavender one." Then sister Coulda agrees that if she had picked the lavender dress, she could have had a dress more suitable for tea as well as for a luncheon. After all, the blue dress is only suitable for tea.

You're probably getting the drift of where I'm going with this. Try to make a mental note of how often you make statements like these: "I should have done this; I could have done that; if things were different, I would have chosen this." This mentality exhibits a lack of acceptance and understanding of the choices we make for ourselves. Often when a situation unfolds that doesn't meet our expectations, we see things differently from the way we did while in the midst of making our decision.

Rather than dwelling on what you should have, would have, and could have done, a better statement to tell yourself is: What I learned from this experience is that the next time I'm faced with a similar set of circumstances and options, I will do things differently. But for now, I will deal with things the way they are.

Questioning oneself can be a healthy part of the growth process. After all, we make thousands of decisions that affect ourselves and those around us daily. If an opportunity arises where a similar set of circumstances are present, you may well make a different choice from what you did before. But when you have regrets about your choices and dwell on them, you aren't necessarily growing, but rather you're wishing things are different from the way they are. Certainly there are times when we know we could have done something differently, but instead of dwelling on what we can't change in our past, we simply need to feel that we have learned something new, and tuck it away for a later date.

So the next time you catch yourself dwelling on your past options, see your silliness and don't go there, girl! Remember that "Shoulda, Woulda, Coulda" doesn't count for much, so place your best foot forward, one step at a time. You can learn your lessons from your perceived mistakes and make a different choice the next time around.

11

SAVE YOUR POT-STIRRING FOR COOKING DINNER

A "pot-stirrer" who is concocting something other than delicious soup is someone who brings up emotional issues that have already been discussed, resolved, or are on their way to being released. She wants to feed the emotional fire and keep it burning for the excitement of the conflict, well beyond the point of being helpful. Pot-stirrers can be subtle; they often even appear to be the "helpful" friend or "caring" listener.

Here's an example: Your friend Joyce comes to you with a problem; she's found out her husband has been cheating on her. She is upset, and she understandably needs your comfort, so of course, you lend her your ear. As time goes on, you have many conversations about the topic of Joyce's husband and what a schmuck he is. Then, months later, Joyce and her husband Bruce are in counseling trying to rebuild their marriage and Joyce's trust. A funny thing happens: You see Joyce one day and she is actually smiling. You begin to ask how things are going with her and Bruce. She tells you that things are better. You say: "How can you possibly trust him when he leaves the house?" By asking this, you cross the line from supportive friend into superb emotional pot-stirrer.

Pot-stirring can take far more subtle forms, as well. It's not just stirring up the big issues, such as infidelity. It occurs every time we encourage someone to get caught up in an issue that is already headed toward a healthy resolution. It's as if we are saying, "Don't let it go! Why would you want to do that? This is too much fun!"

You've just let go of a minor conflict with your neighbor, when your other neighbor continues to bring up how annoying this person is, encouraging you to stay immersed in your irritation. The same applies at work. A coworker can't stop reminding you that it was you, not Gail, who really deserved the credit for that great idea. Every time she says it, your stomach grabs you and your wound opens again.

The trick is to be able to recognize a pot-stirrer, and as well, to save your own pot-stirring for cooking dinner. When someone else is stirring up your pot, see it as a habit that can't harm you unless you engage in the conversation or encourage it in some way. A simple way to disengage is to remember that you've already let go of the issue, and to say so.

There's no question that the temptation to stir the pot is there. In fact, I'll admit to stirring a few pots that had nothing to do with dinner, myself. However, ultimately, pot-stirring is in no one's best interests. It causes unnecessary angst and stress. So, remind yourself that to stir the pot is counterproductive to your own peace of mind and to the resolution of your issues. It's like choosing to overcook your evening meal—all you end up with is burnt soup!

12

SPEAK FROM YOUR LOVE

Are you one of those ever-patient souls who never loses her temper, never erupts like a hot volcano? Do you always speak to your children, spouse, and friends from a calm and loving place in your heart? If you answered yes to these questions, go ahead and skip this strategy. Otherwise, read on.

The key to speaking from your love is first locating and honoring your love, and then knowing when you're not acting from it. When you're in touch with your heart, you feel a connection with others and you have access to your wisdom. You can discuss any feelings from this heart-space, which is quiet and exudes peace, compassion, and understanding. It's that place in you that wells up with tears of joy while you are watching a child innocently at play. It's where you truly feel your emotions. On the other hand, discussing the smallest of issues (like who's going to take out the trash) when you're not connected to your heart, is often problematic and stressful.

Why, then, does it become difficult for all of us, at times, to be in touch with the most magnificent part of who we are—our love—and then to speak from this place? Our egos and emotions and habits of reacting and overreacting keep us from speaking from our love.

It is most challenging to speak from your love when you are angry.

Your feelings of anger can become your best reminder to first get in touch with your heart before you utter a word. Pay attention to your feelings. Be aware of the part of you that wants to lash out, scream, and shout! This is clearly a warning to catch your breath and calm down; you are not in your heart-space; you are preparing to speak from your anger.

It is, after all, not what you say, but the feeling that comes through what you say that is usually most important. The same words may have a very different tone based on where you speak from and your feelings when you say them. For example, the statement, "I need to speak with you," could be a new beginning for a couple or the beginning of the end of a relationship, depending upon how this message is delivered.

My own best example comes in my communication with my children. It is especially difficult to remember to speak from my love when my hot spots are pushed. The depth of feeling I have for my kids is like a never-ending well of love that runs to my very core. This deep well is what I must feel first before I speak. Just as I would draw up water from an actual well, I try to bring up my words from that well of love, even when I'm angry or tired. As I choose my words, I may need to pause before I speak. I should ask myself: "Am I about to speak from my love, or from my anger?" If the answer is that I'm about to speak from my anger, it's best to stay calm and tell my kids that I'm not in the right space to talk to them right now. (Besides, they may sweat a little, which can't hurt, while they wait for my return.)

Yet, even knowing this, there are still times when I fly off the handle at them in a purely reactive state of mind and say things that are not loving, which I later regret. During those times, I simply haven't remembered or taken the time to locate my feelings of love before I speak. If I have forgotten and end up speaking from a place of anger or frustration, in a sense my words are lost—it's no surprise they don't hear a word I say.

It feels wonderful when I speak from my love, as I am honoring what is truly inside of me at the heart level, uncluttered and unmuddled with my ego. I am also honoring the person I address with the deepest level of understanding. As you speak to anyone from this place, there is no greater service you can accomplish (except perhaps learning to listen from your love). So, remember, the next time you are in conflict, find that place in your heart and speak from your love.

13

LISTEN FROM YOUR LOVE

As we discussed in the previous chapter, your love is located in your heart. It is from this place we should not only speak, but listen and hear non-defensively what is said to us. It is when you are not in touch with your heart, but instead your ego, that what others say to you affects you negatively. The words you hear become entrenched in your emotional responses of insecurity, anger, resentment, and depression. As you learn to listen from your love, you will hear the ring of truth or untruth in what is said to you, from a place where you are connected to your spirit.

When two people engage in healthy communication from their hearts, we call this a "heart-to-heart." Both people stay open at the heart level and are committed, no matter what is said, remaining detached from their egos. This is the most rich and gratifying form of communication, but the critical inch in the success of a "heart-to-heart" is listening from your love. Once your ego gets the best of you and you become reactive and defensive, the "heart-to-heart" is over.

I remember, several years back, a potential and possibly pivotal moment in Richard's and my relationship where we had a "heart-to-heart." In hindsight, I'm sure glad it turned out to be a "heart-to-heart," because it wasn't necessarily planned that way. Richard came to me, very frustrated about a number of issues in our married life. Even though I was surprised he was feeling these things, a little voice inside me warned that what he wanted right now, in this moment, was to be heard, and that I'd better listen. Fortunately, in that moment I reminded myself of my love for him, and I was able to hear his words detached from my ego. I listened from my love, and he settled down, once he felt heard. Because he felt heard from my heart, he also renewed his love for me. I heard some truth in what he said (at least 50 percent, anyway), and we were able to discuss, with very level heads and without defensiveness, the issues he brought up.

A magical thing always happens when two people communicate from heart to heart. The very issues that were causing emotional distance actually end up pulling the couple closer together to create a deeper intimacy. This is when conflict is actually healthy.

An often difficult time to listen from your heart is when you are at work. You probably think that you would seem like a pushover if you listened in this way on the job. On the contrary, as you listen from your heart, instead of from your ego, your wisdom kicks in and also creates better understanding. The limits you set with people have a much greater impact if they are coming from the right place. And, let's face it, there's room for a few egos to step aside in the workplace! Ego-based communication is highly conflict-oriented and not very productive.

The next time you are in conflict, practice speaking from your love, and don't forget to listen from the same place. Set your ego aside and have a "heart-to-heart." You'll walk away from what could have been a hurtful situation with positive feelings.

14

LOOK IN THE MIRROR

When you think about it, isn't it easier to see another's faults and emotional blind spots than to see your own? We have, however, a built-in mechanism that can point us in the right direction when we're trying to pinpoint our own faults.

Does a talk show host, a girlfriend, or a sister act in a way that irritates you? Or perhaps the way she carries herself bothers you, or you don't like her perfectionist attitude or any other specific personality trait. Chances are, these qualities are ones that you don't like in yourself. It takes tremendous courage and insight to look in the mirror at yourself and see through to the inside, since we are so good at hiding the parts of us that seem too painful to acknowledge.

Let's say you're having a conversation with your best friend. You begin to put down a mutual acquaintance for her shopaholic tendencies and her flamboyant personality. You see her every time you're out shopping, so she has to be out there more than you are. (At this moment, your friend is thinking, "I don't think so.") Later, as your husband cringes at yet another credit card bill that overextends you both financially, you try to tell yourself that you're more in control than the acquaintance you derided earlier. This is the time to take a good look in the mirror.

It's impossible to see something in someone else unless you yourself have the same quality. There is not a person in your life who isn't here to teach you something about yourself. In this way, we act as a constant reflection to one another, and ironically, the more you recoil at something you see in someone else, the more you need to look deep in yourself for this same quality. It may be masked, but it's there. This is the growth process; once you see it, you can make a change and release it!

It's common to point out what we don't like about other people before we take a good look in the mirror and admit that we see these flaws in ourselves. Let's not forget the fact, however, that all is not lost; the opposite is also true. When you recognize another person's higher qualities of compassion, sensitivity, honesty, or integrity, most likely you share these traits and values.

The truth of the matter is that none of us have it "all" together—it's just much easier to see the insecurities and foibles in others than to admit them to ourselves. As you dare to look in the mirror, and see yourself with the clear vision that your thoughts about others can give you, you will become more compassionate and forgiving. Better yet, if personal growth and perspective is something you value, you will reach new heights of awareness, and what you see in the mirror will reflect the understanding and love that you have for yourself and for others. There is no perfect person on the planet. A favorite saying of mine is that we are all perfect in our imperfection, just the way we are.

15

GO WITH THE TWISTS AND TURNS

While it may be true that we feel we can map out every aspect of our lives, occasionally we get thrown a curve ball that wasn't in our plan at all. Life can seem very unpredictable at times; it may feel that you are flying by the seat of your pants, with little control over the outcome of certain events. And, sometimes, what appears to be a negative on the surface may later turn out to be the very stepping-stone of your success.

Often, we hear a success story that begins with: "It was by total accident that I stumbled onto this business." Keeping this in mind, if you look at life as a schoolground with a bit of adventure along the way, and if you have faith that things will work out for the best in the end, you can see the twists and turns in your personal biography as part of what's in store for your greater life plan.

As you begin to see the twists and turns—those surprising events and circumstances that happen for a reason you are not yet aware of—you'll realize that everything that happens to you is part of a perfect plan designed especially for your personalized, Life 101 course. However, you may not always be clear about the purpose of these unplanned, seemingly mistimed events. Your choice is either to doom yourself in the gloom and misery of uncertainty, or to forge ahead and maintain the optimistic attitude that things can only get better from here. Instead of looking forward or backward, anticipating the worst, keep your attention in the here and now, so that you can be open to whatever opportunities present themselves.

As I look back on my life, there were many twists and turns that I now see clearly turned out for the best. For instance, while living in the dormitory at Pepperdine, our floor had a fire. No one was injured, but myself and seven other suitemates lost everything we had brought to school, which at the time was everything I owned. While many of my friends were completely flipped out, oddly enough, I wasn't upset by this fact. I had a feeling that all would work out for the best, even though I was wearing the only clothing I now owned, I had $127 in my checking account, and I had finals in three weeks!

Interestingly, when I called my parents to tell them the news of the fire, my dad shared another twist with me: he had just lost his job. It certainly didn't appear to be good timing, but, as it turned out, my insurance settlement covered all of my itemized belongings, and much of that went toward paying my tuition for the next year. If the fire hadn't happened, I would have had to have dropped out of school and moved back home for lack of finances to continue my education.

You never know when you lose your job, break up with a boyfriend, or miss that flight, what's really in store for you. You may very well be on the cusp of a career or job change that alters your financial future, or you may meet your soulmate. Part of the adventure in life is not always knowing what's going to happen next, and the next part may be grander than your original plan. The key to enjoying the journey is being open to the unknown.

16

HAVE A BOSOM BUDDY

This strategy first came to my attention during Breast Cancer Awareness Week, and I can tell you firsthand that it works! It is sometimes difficult to follow our doctor's orders, and having a buddy can help to motivate us to follow through on tests that we are not looking forward to.

My doctor asked me to get a baseline mammogram two years ago. Did I do it? No. He asked me to get one last year, and again I put it on the back burner. Recently, a dear friend of mine called me to tell me she had found a lump in her breast and needed to get a mammogram. Well, I really wanted to offer to take her, so I called the imaging consultant and asked for an appointment. I explained that I had to come in at the same time as my friend because she was my bosom buddy. The receptionist loved that, and was able to work me in.

When I picked up my friend, we were both a little jittery. You hear all these scary stories, and frankly, we were both wondering if we had enough breast tissue to screen. Well, let me tell you, just don't forget to look down while your breast is smashed flat as a pancake. This gave me a whole new perspective on the modest handful I have!

Anyway, I stripped down and went first and eased the way for my friend. She was wondering why she could hear me laughing all the way in the other room. It took about five minutes for the two of us, and it didn't hurt a bit. Better yet, my friend found out that her lump was nothing but a normal mass of tissue; definite cause for celebration! We then enjoyed a nice lunch, and as we laughed about our experience, my friend told me I knew how to make something uncomfortable a whole lot of fun.

So make an annual date with your best friend to go for a mammogram together. It's a great way to get something done that's potentially un-pleasant, and to give each other support in what can be a stressful time.

17

CREATE MEMORIES FOR
YOUR CHILDREN

Life is filled up with a lot to do. We can become lost in the task of day-to-day living and just getting here and there. It seems that our children are losing their childhoods too quickly in our efforts to meet the demands of a busy world.

A strategy that helps me to slow down is to think in terms of creating memories for my children. It helps to frequently ask yourself the question: "How do I want my kids to remember their childhoods, and what do I really want for them anyway?"

Whether you're a working mom or a stay-at-home mom or all of the above, often it's the mother in the household whose job it is to bring tradition and ritual into your home. Holidays are great occasions on which to create such memories.

In our family, Christmastime is, by far, our most special and traditional time. It was the same in my own home growing up. I have fond memories of midnight church service, caroling at old folks' homes, decorating cookies, and trimming the tree. Other families have special Kwanzaa and Hanukkah traditions at this time of year. No matter what your religion or background, recreate the traditions your parents observed to carry on their values and treasured memories.

Every year our family goes to a country road tree farm and picks out our tree. We bring it home, put Christmas tunes on the CD player, and trim it with ornaments while we enjoy hot chocolate. We spend Christmas day with cousins and grandparents.

Apart from the holidays, think of simple things to do on the weekends as a family. Hiking is free, and exploring on foot provides for great nature walks. My kids love to take a bag and collect things as they go. Then they come home and create an art project by building a collage. We do the same thing in the spring as we go on newt walks to see the little lizards that come out after the rain, or go on wildflower searches.

The next time your kids come into the house with muddy shoes and dirty clothes, before you get miffed at the extra work they just created for you, think of the fun they had getting that way. Clothes and shoes are replaceable; memories are not.

"Game night" is also a great deal of fun. Play games like Monopoly, go fish, Yahtzee, or dominoes with your kids. Children love nothing more than to sit around a fire and play a game or read a story; it's not really what you do, it's that you are doing it together as a family. I believe that kids remember the "feeling" of the activity as much or more than the specific activity itself. So have fun, be enthusiastic, and create good feelings as a family.

As your children grow up, find a way to record the good times. Scrapbooking is a wonderful creative outlet, and it helps your children remember those events that you've recorded.

Childhoods are fleeting, and we only get one shot at them. If you create memories for your children, you will find fulfillment in the joy of knowing you are giving them a most precious and priceless gift.

18

BE REFLECTIVE

To be a reflective person is to be spiritually rich. It is to acknowledge that there is room for growth and change in our lives, and that there's something to be gained by all of our experiences. The reflective mind sees the possibilities in life and searches for new meaning and ways to do things—especially when something isn't working the way we are already going about it. I'd like to share with you how simple it is to become more reflective and how you can see solutions to problems more clearly by doing so.

The key element to being more reflective is learning to quiet your mind. You can do this in many simple ways. Think of taking the noise away and softening the busy chatter in your mind. This can come through quiet time spent exercising, meditating, in prayer, or any activity which is quiet time spent alone. As soon as you open to your reflective mind and quiet down, the answers or growth you are searching for will begin to flow.

What's in it for you to be a more reflective person? A lot!

The reflective person opens up her inner world and embarks on the greatest adventure that life has to offer—getting to know and understanding oneself. The quality of being reflective best puts to use our gift of female intuition and is the cornerstone to personal growth. It is exciting, empowering, and incredibly liberating to realize that your own mind holds the lock and the key to your mental health and well-being. You can alter yourself, through personal reflection, to make your life better, thereby affecting everyone else positively. Being a reflective person will help you in all arenas of your life, and is a quality of great humility. Every relationship you have benefits from your ability to step back from yourself, and from your courage to examine your own contribution to your problems.

I'm sure you've heard it said, if you haven't said it a time or two yourself: Every story has at least two sides. A person who is not in a reflective state of mind lacks the ability to see her contribution to any given conflict. In fact, she's downright difficult in relationships for this reason. She's not open to hearing any truth in what you may have to say, which makes communication a complete waste of time and energy.

It's important to set aside some reflective time on a daily basis. This can be accomplished by spending time alone in quiet and solitude. Even fifteen minutes at any point during the day can make a world of difference.

Nurture your reflective mind by questioning yourself at times when your mind is quiet. Be humble and ask your inner self if there are any insights or new ways of seeing things that can help you grow as a person or make your life a little easier or more effective. My guess is that you will be amazed at the doors that will open and the answers you'll find!

19

STRESS-BUSTERS

We all have days in which we feel exhausted and stressed out. I'd like to share with you a few ideas that help me to cope and to stop sweating the small stuff. I hope that they will help you in some small way, too.

- Create a ritual in the morning or evening of having at least ten minutes of quiet time. Sit comfortably with a cup of coffee or tea, or close your eyes and listen to quiet music. Or, better yet, meditate, pray, or just breathe. If you have children, get up a little earlier, or stay up after you put them to bed. This will give you the well-deserved downtime you need, and your frenzied pace will feel eased.

- After a nice, long hot bath, wash your hair and rinse your head in cool water. This is one of the most simple and refreshing things you can do to bring your energy up. The contrast between the cool water running through your scalp and the warm water in which your body is immersed is amazing. No matter how tired I am when I get in, I am always ready to rock when I get out.

- On the days when my kids are going crazy and not getting along, instead of being totally reactive with them, I'll tell them, "Mom is taking a time-out!" Then, I do just that. I remove myself from them and ask them to please not cause permanent harm to each other (which they have never come close to doing).

- Do something physical nearly every day. I run, ride my horse, hike, stretch, or lift weights. Even when I'm pressed for time, I squeeze one or two of these activities into my daily schedule. Not only are the physical benefits outstanding, but the mental health and clarity you feel is irreplaceable.

- Lose yourself in a good book from time to time. Even if it's only for twenty minutes a night before you go to sleep, reading can be a relaxing escape—and it sure beats the nightly news for reducing stress.

- If you've been sitting at your computer or desk for too long, your neck and back muscles can become cramped and tired. Every hour or so, stand up, slowly curl your back down and reach for your toes, keeping your legs fairly straight, then curl your back slowly up again. Reach for the sky, then repeat.

- Consider that one of the reasons you may be feeling so stressed is that you're physically out of balance. It's more difficult to feel content and happy if your system is toxic. When I feel this way, I like to have a "health binge." I cleanse by eating very "alive" (i.e., fresh) fruits, veggies, and juices for at least three days. This helps me to break the cycle of some of the unhealthy eating habits I have temporarily adopted, and balances my approach to healthy eating.

These relaxation techniques are very simple, but really work well. Practicing one or two of these each day can really make a difference in your stress levels. I encourage you to give them a try. You'll find it much easier to not sweat the small stuff!

20

PERHAPS IT'S NOT PERSONAL

If there's one thing that many women have in common, it's our sensitive natures. Along with this quality comes a tendency to internalize and impute meaning and motive to the behavior and actions of others. Here's a thought: rather than going with your immediate reaction, consider that, at least some of the time, the things that happen really have nothing to do with you, personally, at all. It just may be that you are trusting the erroneous thoughts and feelings that have warped your perception, rather than admitting to yourself that perhaps it's not personal. Let me give you a few scenarios that might seem familiar.

You have an acquaintance that you've met in school through your kids. Every time you see her, she doesn't even acknowledge you. In fact, she seems to look right past you. You begin to feel uncomfortable, thinking, "What's her problem, anyway?" You start to get mad, as she obviously thinks she's too good for you. But have you considered the possibilities that could easily explain her apparent standoffishness? Maybe she's nearsighted. Maybe she doesn't make eye contact because she doesn't have time to socialize. Maybe she has other things on her mind. Maybe she's thinking the same thing about you. Just maybe, it's not personal.

Your spouse gets home and is in a low mood. He's been putting out fires all day. You've put out a few of your own today, as well, and you were looking forward to an enthusiastic reception. Instead, he retreats to his office, grumbling that he's not hungry for dinner, he has too much work still to do. Need I say more? Rather than blow up and have a nasty confrontation, consider that perhaps it's not personal. He's simply had a bad day.

Taking things personally only causes you unnecessary frustration, while leaving other people baffled by your reactions. We've temporarily attached our self-worth to another person's apparent actions and motives.

It's helpful to step back and see the bigger picture. We need to have a bit more self-preservation and higher self-esteem than that. We need to break the habit of overreacting because of our speedy assumptions and judgments. So the next time you catch yourself annoyed at a person or situation, remember to say to yourself: "Perhaps it's not personal—and so what if it is!"

21

DON'T LET THE MEMBERS OF
YOUR FAMILY DODGE YOUR DRAFT

My friend called me up frustrated, saying that she felt like a horse without a cart! She wished someone in her family besides her would take some initiative to contribute to the household responsibilities. This is a fair request, but one that's not easy to implement. At the same time, you might not want your role as majordomo of the household threatened, or to feel inadequate because you're asking for help. (Hogwash on that anyway! Of course you need help! There's just one of you—you're out-numbered!) Although, if you're anything like me, it's always been easier to "just do it" than to nag someone else.

The problem with this kind of "I'll do it all myself" mentality is that as your children turn into young adults, they don't get any neater, and their messes don't get any smaller; they become grown-up-sized. More important, by doing everything for them, unseen and unappreciated, you are not encouraging them to be self-reliant or teaching them responsibility. You are not preparing them to be adults. Before they are capable of taking care of someone else someday, they first have to learn to take care of themselves.

Even if you are lucky enough to afford weekly housecleaning help, daily picking-up is usually called for to keep your house organized and clean. Your best strategy is to enlist your family members and make the announcement at your next family meeting: "Mom's calling the draft, and any dodgers don't get new school clothes or anything extra!" (then define what "extra" means). It doesn't hurt to let your kids know what is expected of them. Then, hand out your list of chores and explain that you plan on rotating them monthly so everyone gets a chance to experience the many aspects of keeping a house clean. You may consider giving your kids an allowance, although, personally, I think kids should get an allowance for their fun stuff, and do their chores as a contribution to their households.

In order for this new enlistment to be effective, you will also have to turn over a new leaf. You'll need to stop the "just do it" philosophy, and instead adopt a "leave it right where it is or throw it in the trash" attitude. You have to be prepared to follow through and issue the consequences that you promised (no new clothes, no extras) for unfinished business. Remember that old habits die hard, so give it a month or so and everyone will adjust fine. Kids are actually a lot happier knowing that they're contributing to their family's well-being, so you're doing them a favor by enlisting their assistance.

22

ENVY NOT

It seems that envy is something that most of us are prone to experience. While envy may be a natural emotion in some ways, it can be so powerful that it grabs hold of you. Envy can easily make you obsess about whatever you are jealous of. It's a very powerful feeling that can drive us to do and think things we might not, otherwise. But by admitting that you struggle with envy, you may be able to free yourself from its limiting grasp.

Paula was a very accomplished film editor who'd been nominated for an award for her work on a well-received documentary. You'd think she would be a self-assured person, but instead she was extremely jealous of other people in her industry, even her friends. She literally couldn't bring herself to congratulate acquaintances on their successes, even though she wasn't in direct competition with them.

Over time, a few close friends as well as some people she greatly respected hinted to Paula that she had a tendency to envy others. As is often the case, the truth was hard to swallow, especially at first. After a bit of honest reflection, however, she was able to admit to herself that she did, indeed, suffer from attacks of the green-eyed monster.

By being honest with herself, Paula began to realize that her fears and jealousies were holding her back both professionally and personally. She realized that envy not only made her look bad, but it made her feel bad, too. She resolved to make an effort to avoid these feelings in the future. It took time, but gradually she became more secure about her own abilities and gave less significance to her comparisons to others. As a result, she became far less envious of others; in fact, she has even learned to be happy for others for the successes they enjoy.

The whole "keeping up with the Joneses" mentality is a common trap that also begins with envy. Your neighbor gets a new car, and all of a sudden your car looks a little bit older. You feel a bit jealous. The important questions are: Do you respond to that emotion with an urgent desire to go right out and buy a new car yourself, whether you need one or not; or do you sit on it for a while? Do you wallow in feelings of self-pity because you can't afford one, or do you attempt to be happy for your neighbor and let go of it?

Your envy can be a great teacher, and can save you a lot of frustration from trying to keep up with others. After all, there's always going to be someone who has more money, prettier hair, a nicer kitchen, who moves up more quickly in their career, etc. If you buy into your envy, you're like a dog chasing its tail, never able to make progress. However, if you're willing to admit your feelings, you'll make your decisions based on what you need and want for personal reasons of satisfaction, and that is so much more rewarding in the long run.

Being able to feel happy about others' good qualities and luck can help you to become a more peaceful person. In fact, it's been said that the ability to be happy for others is a sign of mental health. When you think about it, being envious is a very stressful emotion. Practice letting go of those feelings of jealousy. You'll find yourself becoming a happier, more satisfied person if you do.

23

FIND YOUR GIFTS AND
SHARE THEM

We are all made of mostly the same stuff, yet each of us has a unique set of gifts and talents that help us to fulfill our special purpose and contribution. Some of us find our talents early in life in the more obvious ways as an athlete, academic, dancer, musician, or artist. And, while one of these may come more easily to one woman, another person's ease in communicating her feelings, for instance, may be more difficult for you. Others may bloom later and find that their gifts are less flamboyant; they may be great in supporting people through excellent listening skills, or they may be a fantastic team player, or a creative entrepreneur, or writer. You may realize that you are a gifted mother, wife, and household manager.

Are our unique gifts those talents we are naturally good at, or are they the things we love to do? Perhaps it's a little of both, but the gifts that come from our passion, and the love in our hearts, are the ones that are ultimately the most powerful.

Giving a gift that we all have access to—the gift of love—is perhaps the most magnificent of all. Love reveals itself in many forms. When you give in a service-oriented way—where you receive nothing extrinsic such as payment, credit, or acclaim—then you also receive a gift in the giving; the joy that comes from the satisfaction of making a loving contribution.

In contrast, turning away from your natural gifts, and instead striving toward a goal in which the requisite skills aren't intrinsic to you, can be very frustrating. For instance, pursuing a career as a dancer if you have two left feet might be more challenging than fulfilling. Conversely, if you have a knack for communication, becoming a computer programmer may be too isolating for your temperament.

How can you identify what your gifts are? Ask your friends and family to help you describe them. What shines about you may be obvious to others, but may not always be as clear to you. It may take some courage and faith for you to find your gifts, and then a little more courage and faith to share them. Follow your heart. The universe has a way of confirming your direction with open doors. Whatever your gifts, each one is valuable; all are equally important to each of us in fulfilling our individual purpose, as well as our own life's lessons.

Your gifts may at first appear to have a single purpose, but later they may play a different role in your life than you initially expected. Many people are blessed with a measure of success, and then give back to the world in the form of supporting a cause they strongly believe in. A great athlete or actress may find that the purpose of her celebrity was not only to serve her own goals, but to also serve a greater cause. Andrea Jaeger, for example, a world-class tennis player in the eighties, found her obvious gifts as an athlete and then lobbied her talents altruistically later. She now finds great purpose in being the founder of the Silver Lining Foundation in Aspen, Colorado, a nonprofit organization which serves children living with cancer. (For more information, contact Chris Wyman, 1490 Ute Avenue, Aspen, CO 81611; phone: 970-925-9540; fax: 970-544-0565; e-mail: www.silverliningfoundation.org)

There are so many gifts people share that may seem invisible, but that have a lasting influence on those around them. In addition, choosing to mentor by example is a great gift to give. Share what you've learned and help others along the way, so they can turn around and do the same thing.

24

TAKE TIME FOR YOUR SELF

Taking time for your self is perhaps the most obvious of all the strategies in this book, yet it may be the most powerful of all, particularly for busy women (and who among us isn't busy?). It seems that, more often than not, time for ourselves becomes the very last priority. Yet, our "to-do" list continues to grow and grow. As we get busier, our priorities get muddled, and we spend less and less time nourishing our inner selves. After a while, it seems we can't even remember what it's like to feel nourished and peaceful.

What we do feel is a sense of urgency. We treat life like an emergency, frantically crossing things off our list, so we can supposedly get it all done. We imagine that we'll take time for ourselves when this happens—and, of course, it never does. We begin to feel as if we're living life like we're a loose cannon, out of control.

If you don't like these feelings (and I've never met a woman who does), you must begin to realize that taking time for yourself is not a selfish, valueless act. On the contrary, you will be amazed at how much more you'll be capable of giving to those around you, and to those you love, as well as what you can accomplish, as you practice nourishing your own spirit first. It doesn't matter if you are a mother, wife, sister, daughter, corporate executive, full-time employee, or all of the above: If you don't take care of your self, you won't have it in you to keep up your current pace. Eventually, you'll simply fall on your face in pure exhaustion. You'll discover that you can't be happy—and you certainly can't give to others—if you have nothing inside left to give.

We all need breaks now and then, such as lunch with a friend, a spa day, an afternoon spent journaling in the park, or having a massage or facial. Everyone also needs an occasional weekend away or vacation. We all need time off, and we all need to have some fun! These are important ways to create a healthy balance and an enjoyable life.

What I'm suggesting, however, is that you take this concept a few steps deeper, in order to find your peaceful center. Unfortunately, an occasional break, spaced weeks or even months apart, only provides a Band-Aid for your sense of being overwhelmed. In order to nourish your deeper needs, it's necessary to take some time each day to rejuvenate and lighten your spirit.

Rather than beginning your day scrambling around at a frenetic, hurried pace, try waking up each day at least fifteen minutes earlier than everyone else and create a ritual of nourishing silence. Meditate or watch the sunrise while sipping your coffee or tea. Or, spend some time in prayer or quiet reflection. As you find your own way to begin each day connecting with your self, you will maintain a reflective, slower pace throughout the day. You'll see what's most important, and, amazing as it may seem, you may even receive insights about what can be cut from your schedule. Although it may be difficult to believe, you'll quickly discover that this is true. The benefits far outweigh the burdens (you won't refer to them in this way for long), and you'll feel better right away.

25

LET OUT YOUR STEAM LIGHTLY

We are creatures of habit. Many of our habits, unfortunately, are quite invisible to us. One that can kill a relationship that might otherwise flourish is the habit of letting your angst grow into a hot air balloon. Keep in mind that it is a lot more healthy for any relationship, and you are more likely to be heard, if you let out your steam lightly in a form of communication that is spoken from compassion—rather than blowing up like a bomb.

Women who keep their anger brewing can be a little like a covert enemy who launches a surprise attack. Whether she is angry at something her partner did last night or two months earlier, she will strike when given the opportunity to vent her stored-up hostility. This is what happens when we fail to face our partner, friend, or family member and say what we are truly bugged about in the moment. If we continue to sweep our irritation under the rug, then eventually, when our mood is low enough, we are sure to blow. The sad thing is, we aren't blowing up at the small thing that just happened; it is the weeks, months, or even years of poor communication about similar issues that has finally made us lose it.

The key is to determine the small stuff you can live with, without sweating it, and the stuff that you really cannot stand. There are certain times of the month that I become more irritated, and I know it is not my life that has changed; only my mood. During these times, when something is bugging me, I know that in another week, the same thing will look totally different to me. I understand that my perspective is tweaked a bit, and I don't take it too seriously. I definitely don't go around broadcasting what I'm thinking.

A friend of mine works at home and has small children. Her husband also works full-time, at home as well, yet all of the household and childcare responsibilities fall on Laurie. On the surface, she takes it in stride, as it seems easier for her to manage everything on her own than to become a nag to George. Under the surface, however, a slow and penetrating resentment grows in her. Laurie does not understand how he can schedule tennis dates and lunches out while she is scrambling to juggle everything at home. The reality is this: Laurie has set up her life this way, and George has no idea that she has these feelings, until one day she comes at him in a blinding rage. Laurie feels that George would have to be deaf, dumb, and blind, not to see all that she does in a day. What she doesn't know is that he sees it, but it has always worked pretty well for him that way, and he doesn't have a clue that she's bothered. Why would he try to fix something that's not broken?

Laurie has failed to let her steam out lightly over the years by setting clear boundaries and renegotiating the ones that no longer work for them as a couple. Family life is about bending and blending, and is full of negotiation. We must be able to say from our heart, "This doesn't work for me any longer, and this is why." (Please see chapters, "Speak from Your Love" and "Listen from Your Love," for more on having a heart-to-heart discussion.) Then, we must be willing to hear the response to what is said without defensiveness.

If your goal is to have a happy household and a good marriage, don't sweat the really small stuff, but do practice better communication. Stop sweeping your frustrations under the rug! You can't expect your partner to read your mind or your actions, either. You have to speak what's on your mind in a gentle way, so that he is able to hear you—then you will let your steam out lightly and avoid the big blows that can leave your relationship damaged with very little change or negotiation accomplished.

26

ACCEPT COMPLIMENTS WITH "THANK YOU"

How many of us actually accept compliments graciously by simply saying "thank you?" Someone praises the good in us, and rather than accepting their praise, for fear that we may seem conceited or lack humility—or perhaps we are truly insecure—we hem and haw and give all the reasons why we aren't worthy of their compliment.

A friend of mine said that an older friend of hers once bestowed the same advice: "You know, Susie, if I tell you I like the color of your hair, or your outfit looks nice, or how much I admire your talent for decorating, don't waste my time by giving me a litany of reasons why I am lying to you. It doesn't encourage me to compliment you in the future." Susie could save both their time and energy, the next time she is complimented by her friend, by replying simply, "Thank you."

If a friend of yours gave you a present for no other reason than to be nice, you wouldn't throw the present back in her face, would you? If you did, I guarantee it would be the last present you received from that friend! Compliments are no different. They are unsolicited gifts of appreciation and acknowledgment. You accept them, in the same way you would accept a present from a friend—with grace.

When you accept a compliment with thanks, it doesn't mean you are conceited, but rather that you have learned a thing or two about grace.

We need to remember that to accept grace with gratitude is to invite divine energy directly to us in the form of a compliment. One of the greatest feelings is to give a heartfelt compliment, knowing that it is received in the same spirit it was given.

The next time someone uses their energy to say something nice to you, enjoy the praise, and save both of your time by replying with a simple "thank you."

27

AVOID CYBER-RIFT!

In today's speedy and often impersonal world, we are able to communicate in ways never before imagined. E-mail has become a very popular form of communication, both for business and with family and friends. There certainly are advantages to e-mail, including efficiency and convenience. Yet, along with those advantages come some potentially stressful if not hurtful disadvantages. One of the disadvantages to be aware of, if you are an "e"-kind of gal, is the potential for something I call "cyber-rift." Simply put, cyber-rift is conflict or tension caused by acting on a negative impulse or the need to express your feelings instantly through e-mail. One impulsive click of the *send* button can harm a relationship or create unnecessary conflict in your life.

When you are sitting at the computer writing an e-mail, it's easy to lose your inhibitions. Because you are alone, sitting in front of a screen, it feels safe to reveal your private thoughts. And because of the impersonal nature of using a keyboard, we can be tempted to write things that we would not otherwise say in person or on the telephone. After all, no one is watching us or listening to us. It's just us and our computer. So we feel safe typing a few thoughts. Perhaps we're a little angry or hurt, or we're in a lousy mood or feeling frustrated. Without even thinking about it, we type out our frustration, maybe say a few mean things. We write down what we really think about someone, or we express some sort of dissatisfaction. Then, boom, in an instant, our feelings are sent through cyber-space. By the time we even realize what we have said, or think through any potential implications, it's too late. The message has been sent; the damage has been done.

Tempting as it may be, it's important to remember that when you're angry, hurried, or feeling reactive, this is not the time to send your thoughts by e-mail. It is always better to wait until you cool off on an issue or gain some perspective before you air what's on your mind. If you feel like writing a letter, go ahead and do so, but write it out longhand or, at the very least, do so when you're not on-line. That way, you will have time to reflect on what you're saying and how it will be received. You can always choose to send the letter later, but at least you'll have the option of not doing so, if you so choose.

I have been surprised at how many men get into cyber-rifts. It seems that some men are better able to communicate their feelings through e-mail, which is, ironically, impersonal. They will spit out everything from profanity, to how busy and tired they are, to all-out insults. Do you think a highly educated man would write a business memo in which he used the f-word, unless he was e-mailing it? I doubt it. Yet there is a way in which e-mail encourages a sort of primitive impulse to emerge.

Although there are probably certain justifiable exceptions, in most cases it's better not to impulsively express your negative feelings through e-mail. The instant gratification you feel will almost always be over-shadowed by the stress you create for yourself and for the recipient of your feelings afterward. I think you'll agree that most cyber-rift is counterproductive, and can be avoided by simply being aware of the problem. As is usually the case, patience serves us well.

28

PROTECT YOUR INNER FLAME

We can best be of service to others if we learn to keep our own emotional well-being intact. Our well-being is a source of strength. It is our peace of mind, inspiration, and natural source of wisdom. On the other hand, if we don't keep our well-being intact, we're not much good to others. After all, it's impossible to give that which we don't have.

Think of your well-being as your own inner flame; it is a candle burning brightly inside of you. This flame is at the core of your being, and when you are feeling quiet and peaceful, your well-being is intact and your candle is burning brightly with ease.

Your sense of well-being is your own special light of peace that you carry inside you; it is also your innate health. Just as you might, occasionally, need to guard a real candle's flame gently with your hand to protect it from the wind, you also want to do the same thing with your well-being. It's important to gently protect your inner flame so it doesn't begin to burn too low. When my well-being is jeopardized, I feel scattered, fatigued, unfocused, and unable to access my inner source of wisdom and peace.

Each of us must find our own way to nourish and strengthen this flame. When mine is low, it is an indication to me that I am super "caught up" in my head. During these times, I realize that I need to insulate and isolate myself for a little while. I need to breathe very deeply and make an attempt to empty my head of the myriad of "small stuff" concerns and pressures that weigh me down and leave me feeling low.

My greatest personal challenge, emotionally, since becoming a mother, has been to try to maintain my own sense of well-being while my children are experiencing a low mood or having an emotional fit. I have noticed, over the years, that it doesn't benefit any of us to have all of us spiraling downward and out of control at the same time! During these times, it's important to protect your inner flame by seeing your children as separate from you; they are their own people, entitled to having their own high and low moods. This is an idea I have found quite challenging at times, but nevertheless important.

The first step in maintaining your own inner peace is to find a way to keep your bearings, stay centered, and to protect the flame inside. It's helpful to be able to recognize when we are caught up in our thinking and are having what Richard calls a "thought attack." By recognizing that your thinking is off, or that you're overly caught up in it, and taking a break or putting a confrontation on hold, your well-being has a chance to bounce back. You will then make the most appropriate decisions about what to say and do.

As you understand the implications of this strategy in your daily life as a woman, friend, mother, spouse, and coworker, you may begin to see it as one of the most important elements of the emotional stability of your family, and to those around you. As you keep your well-being intact, you will find yourself better able to serve your friendships, as well as to be more compassionate and caring with your spouse and everyone you are in contact with. The trick is to see the relationship of your own thinking to the power behind your flame, and to realize that when your flame is low, you are not capable, emotionally, to deal with a problem. It is much easier to experience the joys in parenting and all of life if we learn to get through the difficult times more gracefully. So, keep that candle burning bright.

29

UNDERSTAND THE DIFFERENCE
BETWEEN INTUITION AND FEAR

What exactly is intuition, and how do we know the difference between intuition and fear? It is important to be aware of the difference so you are able to use the gift of intuition to help guide your life. Differentiating between the two allows you to piece together information to help you make decisions. It will keep you from being reactive, and from making your decisions from a place of irrational fear. Your intuition can also help you to use fear in a healthy way to keep yourself and others safe from harm. It is important to pay heed to your intuitions; they are often right on target.

The easiest way to tell the difference between fear and intuition is to recognize the very subtle difference between the two. While all feelings come first from our thoughts, intuition is a strong feeling, like a sixth sense we have, where there is no fear present at the onset. An intuitive feeling almost seems to dangle in the air; it's what many describe as a "gut" feeling. You feel strongly about something, and then you think about how you feel. It could be a feeling of unease or distrust, or a strong sense of anticipation or a good omen. At times, something just simply feels "right."

Fear makes itself known as a fearful feeling that immediately stems from a fearful thought. Without question, it starts in your head, as the fearful thought comes first. The true difference between fear and intuition is that you are usually aware of what you are afraid of, therefore having a concrete image in your mind. However, when your intuition is at work, you may not be able to put your finger on what you are anticipating.

If you're always afraid to get on an airplane, or you're in the habit of thinking perilous thoughts prior to flying, then this is probably not intuition at work. However, if you are usually not afraid of flying and all of a sudden have a gripping intuition about getting on an airplane, it might be a good idea to listen to that feeling. In this instance, your intuition may be speaking to you.

I can tell the difference between my own intuition and fear with a very simple observation about my own psyche. My fears come up often, but my intuition speaks to me more rarely, and seems to come from nowhere. For example, on the mornings my running partner is not available, I frequently have safety concerns about running alone. I know this is fear because I have noticed my own personal thought pattern. While I don't let this stop me from running alone, I may decide to alter my route if I see someone or something on the trail that does not feel right to me.

There is a time and a place for a little healthy fear, especially if your intuition isn't kicking in or you are unsure about it. Fear is an emotion that keeps us safe when applied with a common sense attitude. After all, without fear, we would throw all caution to the wind as if we were invincible. However, like any emotion, when our fear becomes unbalanced, it becomes destructive. It then works as an irrational force in our lives, and can play havoc with our health, both physically and mentally.

I like to think of our intuition as the ability to tune into our own innate wisdom; our "higher self" or the part of us that is connected to our spiritual center. We need to develop a keen sense of our intuition, and this can take practice. Meanwhile, notice the subtle difference between your intuition and your fear. If you do, you will always come from a place of strength when making important decisions, whether big or small.

30

SET CLEAR BOUNDARIES

Fortunately, we have long ago relinquished the image of "the submissive woman." For many of us, though, it's a struggle to make our needs and limits known to the people we work with, as well as the people we live with. Yet if we can learn to set clear boundaries, we will avoid letting people take advantage of us, as well as offset many feelings of frustration.

Before you are able to set boundaries with others, you must first be clear on what your personal boundaries are. You must know your bottom line; feelings of anger and resentment help you to define what that is. Whether it's with your husband, coworkers, children, in-laws, or parents, setting clear boundaries ensures better communication. Less of the small stuff will frustrate you because the people you are in relationships with will know where you stand.

Ann, who is married to Tom, did not realize how important it was to have boundaries, much less set them with her husband. Her thoughts about love went something like this: If you truly love someone, you give them whatever they want, attempt to fill all of their needs, and always offer them complete compassion and understanding, even if they fail you miserably in their ability to stay committed to you. While, in theory, these are ideals worth pursuing, they will only work if they are completely reciprocated by both parties. If not, then the one who has been doing all the giving will eventually realize that they are getting the short end of the stick and become angry and resentful. After seven years of marriage, Ann began to feel like Tom's doormat.

It wasn't until after she found out that Tom had been unfaithful to her that she really acknowledged her many feelings about their relationship. They had two young children she was busy caring for, and he, in reality, resembled a visiting dad. He always had some excuse about why he was unable to get home before they went to bed.

Ann's anger and resentment told her that her bottom line was that Tom had to break off the relationship with the other woman, and swear that he'd never be unfaithful again. In addition, he needed to be home at least two nights a week by dinnertime. The fact that he had been unfaithful was symptomatic of the lack of communication and intimacy they shared as a couple. And, the truth was, Tom had little respect for Ann. In order to regain his respect as well as her own, Ann had to make it clear to him that she was willing to walk out of their marriage unless he had a change of heart and was willing to make some major changes in his behavior and habits.

Ann and Tom's relationship reveals what happens when you don't set personal boundaries. Ideally, two people in a relationship of any kind would be able to sit down and negotiate their boundaries together. These could relate to financial issues, family matters, sexual issues, how much time you want to spend together, etc. Realize that over time, these boundaries are most likely going to change. Good communicators know how to say, lovingly, "This doesn't work for me anymore . . . and here's why." If you learn to set clear boundaries, you'll reduce the stress in your life that comes from resenting people who overstep their bounds.

Setting clear boundaries is not about being a self-centered person. To be effective, the limits must be reasonable, fair, and not heavily weighted on one side. A friend of mine stated it beautifully when she said, "If your relationship is a fragile bird that you hold in your hand, then you must be careful not to hold the bird so tightly you squeeze the life out of it. Also, you can't hold the bird too loosely or it will fly away. You have to hold it just right."

31

LET GO OF YOUR
"PERFECT" PLANS

You decide to have a party to celebrate your father's sixtieth birthday, or your parents' golden fiftieth wedding anniversary, or perhaps you're planning a neighborhood barbecue. Or, maybe you just want to get away for a romantic weekend.

Whatever the occasion, you embark upon your planning with pure determination that it will be "the perfect day" and you will have the "perfect party."

Unfortunately, as you've undoubtedly already experienced, these "expectations" are surefire, 100 percent guaranteed to at best ensure your disappointment; at median to be a highly stressful experience; and at worst, to give you the beginning of an ulcer.

If you would like to ensure a great party where you also end up enjoying the whole experience, remember to do your best in planning the details, but at the same time, let go of your "perfect" plans. Make allowances, up front, for the fact that there are twists and "speed bumps" in all plans. No matter how attentive you are to details and regardless of your ability to anticipate problems, there's always going to be something you didn't plan. Knowing this in advance is a tremendous source of stress prevention.

We place a tremendous amount of unnecessary pressure on ourselves by having too-high expectations. If you're a perfectionist, this strategy will apply to you doubly. It's helpful to come to peace with the fact that there are too many variables that are out of your control whenever you plan an event. I have yet to hear of a person who can control the weather, how much Uncle Jim drinks that night, or some of the weird family dynamics that are all but certain to occur.

A good indication that your expectations may be running a little high lies in how you are treating your family, caterer, and friends right before the big event. If you are short-tempered, flustered, and snappy, and your face breaks out, chances are, it's time to throw your hands in the air and remember that the party will go on even if you're stressed out! Take a moment to breathe and to lighten up. Try to remember that your initial motivation for planning this occasion came from the inspiration to celebrate and have some fun.

Here's another scenario that never seems to fail: you plan an incredibly romantic weekend away with your husband, forgetting to plan around the one thing that can truly botch it up in a big way. Then, bingo! The day you leave, you get your period. This has happened to me several times. It can be a bummer, but if you can keep your sense of humor and be a little flexible, you can always manage to have a great time anyway.

When something like this happens to us, we simply let go of our original "perfect plan" and go for "Plan B," which includes backrubs, footrubs, long intimate walks on the beach, or in the woods. Deep conversation and candlelit baths become the focus of the weekend. The only time we've failed to have a good time together is when one or the other of us gets too uptight about our "perfect plan."

On a grander life scale, the same strategy applies. If you think you can map out the perfect life and expect that all will stick to your plan, well, good luck. Some things will turn out as you desired, while others will not. We rarely plan to get ill, or fired, or to have to move suddenly for a job.

Often we plan around our expectations of what marriage will be like, or what it will be like once a baby is born. Some of it will turn out as we thought, while much of it will be different from our expectations. The question is how invested you are in the idea that things have to turn out according to your plan. The more invested in your expectations, the more disappointment you will feel when those expectations don't turn out as planned.

One way to look at it is this: Instead of being upset when things don't go according to plans, instead be pleasantly surprised when, once in awhile, something you plan actually meets your expectations! Then, you'll be able to enjoy an event, either way. You'll know that things will be "perfect" just the way they are!

32

DON'T LET SELF-DOUBT STAND
IN YOUR WAY

None of us feel 100 percent confident about all that we are doing 100 percent of the time. If you do, perhaps you aren't pushing your limits enough. While a little bit of self-doubt is healthy and shows us we are stretching ourselves a bit, too much can paralyze our ability to move forward and render us unable to accomplish our goals.

There have been many times in my life when I experienced self-doubt at a healthy level, and, at times, to a degree where it kept me from accomplishing what I set out to do. In all cases I was stretching my capabilities further than I was accustomed, therefore propelling myself toward growth.

If you submit to insecurity and allow self-doubt to grow, it may become bigger than you. You may end up defeating yourself with too much negative thinking. Instead, it's helpful to realize that our doubts are only an internal mechanism to show us that we are out of our comfort zone. There is nothing wrong with feeling a bit uncomfortable. In fact, it is when you are uncomfortable that you may be approaching an incredible opportunity for growth. You can choose not to continue on the same line of negative thinking. Think of it sort of like this: You are playing Monopoly and you land in jail. You draw a chance card which reads, "Pay fifty dollars and get out of jail, or stay in jail three turns." Understanding that you have doubts is your "chance card." Feeding your insecurities with more of the same is like electing to skip three turns, for a measly fifty bucks!

Try to view self-doubt as nothing more than a hiccup; a simple reminder that you're pushing yourself and expanding your potential by doing so. The next time you experience self-doubt, try to see how you're stretching yourself, and welcome the opportunity for growth.

33

GIVE YOURSELF THE GIFT
OF FORGIVENESS

There are times for each of us when we are wronged by someone we trusted, whether it is a friend, lover, or even a family member. And there's no question about it: When this happens, it hurts. Yet, as I see it, we have two choices: We can either be like a hermit crab holding on for dear life inside its shell, or we can give ourselves the freedom of a bird in flight through the gift of forgiveness.

The concept of forgiveness is a challenging one when you think in terms of forgiving the person with whom you are upset. However, the act of forgiveness actually releases you from the damaging effects of your anger and hostility on your own psyche, as well as on your physical well-being. Your emotions are yours; they belong only to you, and have no effect on the person you're angry with.

Forgiveness is a very personal inner task. It is not about telling the person, or offering it to them; in fact, it's not essential to make this person know that he or she has your forgiveness. Instead, it's about opening your heart and freeing your mind from the resentment and hatred you feel. We've all had the experience of deluding ourselves into thinking that evil thoughts give us some sort of revenge. The truth of the matter is, however, that when we feed these kinds of thoughts and emotions, they do nothing more than lock us into an unhealthy state of mind. When you forgive a wrongdoing, you give yourself peace of mind; you can go about your life with feelings of serenity and gratitude again.

I once read an article about a young Korean woman who survived the bombing of her village during war. She escaped with her clothes burned from her body, but her entire family perished in the blaze. While it took years of plastic surgery to heal the wounds of her body, she explained that her true healing occurred when she was able to heal the wounds of her heart by forgiving an entire nation. If one person can forgive an entire nation, can't we forgive one act by one person at a time? I know we can.

We also need to forgive ourselves when we wrong someone else; this can be as difficult for us to do as forgiving someone for hurting us. It is important to acknowledge that our humanness makes us imperfect by nature, and as long as you are alive, you will make mistakes—albeit fewer as you learn from your past lessons. Learning to let go of guilt and forgiving yourself is part of emotional growth. Don't be afraid to ask for forgiveness, either.

The measure of love that you give yourself and others will be in how well you are able to let go of the wrongs of others against you, as well as the mistakes that you make. As you see that your feelings of anger, hatred, bitterness, and betrayal belong only to you, you will see the enormous emotional benefits of giving yourself the gift of peace and serenity which comes only through forgiveness.

34

BE REAL

Here's something fun to think about! Get off the Channel One bandwagon, and try being real on for size. Richard and I first heard this term expressed by philosopher Ram Dass. We have since referred to "Channel One" as the kind of shallow communication many people engage in—e.g., "How's the weather, and what designer clothes are you wearing?"

Channel One communication focuses on things like what kind of car you drive, how much money you make, or what someone looks like. It's not bad or wrong to communicate on Channel One. We all do it and, at times, it's absolutely appropriate. The problem is, if Channel One is all there is, or if you rarely go to "deeper channels," the feelings and interactions you experience won't be as rich and fulfilling as they might otherwise be. You'll feel as though something is missing. There will be a lack of depth, intimacy, and connection in your life.

It's far more nourishing to "be real" and to relate to people in more than just a superficial manner. You do this by opening up, speaking from your heart, being very honest, and asking in-depth questions.

If you spend your energy trying to convince people that you are perfect and never cop to the imperfect aspects of your life, or if you focus only on "Channel One" topics in your interactions, you will eventually find yourself surrounded by people who have also convinced themselves that everything in their world is just "perfect" or who tend to focus mostly on superficial topics. You'll end up feeling isolated, undernourished, and completely alone in a crowded room filled with Channel One types. It's a shallow existence, and one where little that is true to the heart is shared.

There's a woman whom I have known for many years. Every time we get together, usually about once or twice a year, our meeting is typically the same. Her initial greeting is very cheery, but clearly limited to Channel One. She smiles and says how perfect everything is. Her father is "wonderful," even after suffering a heart attack. She is doing just "great," even though her dream is to stay home to raise her three children, yet she finds herself working full-time. Her marriage is "fabulous," despite the fact that living with her husband is like caring for a fourth child.

The problem is, there's really nowhere to go with a conversation like that. And while there's nothing wrong with a Channel One conversation, perhaps a deeper, more honest response would be: "You know, Kris, generally I am a very happy person, but, like everyone else, I do have a few frustrations in my life." This response would open the door and foster a deeper connection between us. It would initiate questions and depth. While we might not get into detail about her frustrations, it would, at the very least, leave me feeling as if she had opened up to me—and would leave her knowing she was being honest.

Of course, there are appropriate places for Channel One types of conversations. You wouldn't get into your personal problems with everyone at your job, for instance, or with people you only know slightly. Sometimes Channel One is good enough. The point is to be able to dance between Channel One and deeper interactions, depending on the situation.

You can be a happy person yet not have a "perfect" life! When your joy is real and comes from your true feelings, let it shine, because you will light up the people around you. When your feelings are phony and you are afraid to be real, you will not relate to people at the heart level, and neither of you will feel nourished.

While it is awesome to share the joy and wonder of life with friends and family, it is isolating to shove the negative feelings under the rug as if you don't have any. As you are able to voice your real feelings about both your happiness and your hardships, and as you feel more comfortable sharing from the heart, you will find that the acknowledgment you receive (from within yourself and from others) will feed your spirit far more than would a Channel One interaction. The acceptance and feeling of closeness you will feel from and toward others will nourish you beyond words. This is the basis of offering unconditional love, as well as opening yourself up to be loved in this way.

35

P.S.—I'M PMS!

I think it would be a good idea if all women had a sign to put on their bedroom doors, which says: P.S.—I'm PMS! On the reverse side it should say: Don't mess with me! Here are my symptoms: frazzled, fizzled, sizzled, dizzy, and very tired. On the bottom, it would say: Handle With Care. The idea would be to give those closest to us a warning and an opportunity to give us some space.

So, with kids, a career, a spouse, and ten pets to care for, how do we get through those PMS days with no casualties? Very carefully.

I have to admit that I'm no joy to be around when in the throes of my PMS. The worst moments are when I blow my stack, then realize that PMS has gotten the best of me. Some rather shocking things come out of my mouth when my system lacks seratonin, and I don't feel myself at all. At least by warning my family that I'm in this phase, they have learned (most of the time) to try to not push my buttons or go overboard in firing requests in my direction.

In my quest to regulate my PMS, I'd like to share a few things that have helped me dramatically. You might give some of these strategies a try:

- Cut back on caffeine intake. Caffeine accentuates the edginess you feel, as well as depletes many of your needed vitamins

- Take a multi-vitamin
- Give in to cravings (but if possible, try not to binge)
- Drink more water and get regular exercise, even though you may feel unusually sluggish
- Take a lot more deep breaths when you are feeling stressed
- Cut yourself some slack; try to create breaks for yourself that allow you to be alone and rest
- Encourage a healthier state of mind by attempting to be more positive
- Realize that your state of mind is not at its best, and therefore put off making major decisions or solving problems until you feel better
- Don't make anything a "big deal." Repeat to yourself over and over, "This, too, shall pass"
- Apologize when you overreact
- Take a more leisurely bath instead of a rushed shower, if at all possible

I hope that you find some of these ideas helpful in getting through a rather challenging physical and emotional part of your cycle. PMS is a real drag, but by being more aware of it, and making a few allowances for the way you feel, you can come to peace with it. Hopefully these tactics will lessen the stress you feel, as well as the amount you take out on those around you.

36

LOWER YOUR THRESHOLD

Women can handle a lot of stress, but is it really in our best interests to have our thresholds so high? I don't think so; generally it backfires on us like an engine that's run out of oil. We don't usually drive our cars until they run out of oil or gas; we get their tanks filled and have them tuned up regularly, maintaining them so they don't conk out on us. In a similar way, we need to avoid taking on more and more stress until we reach the breaking point from all the pressure. If we can take the time and attention to maintain our cars, can't we maintain our stress levels so that we don't take on too much for any one human being?

There are many times I have thought that children should come with some kind of booklet of instructions. In my efforts to be the most patient (which has never been one of my strong points) and loving mother, I used to allow my threshold for tolerating stress to be too high.

I realized that it didn't matter to my children how long they misbehaved or pushed until they found my limit, but it certainly mattered to me. Mistakenly, I thought that "love" meant that my limit had to be high. I would be tolerant until about 5 A.M., then I'd blow like an erupting volcano.

After seeking some guidance from a more experienced source, I had the insight that it wasn't about being patient all day. It was about being patient and setting limits earlier. After all, my daughters weren't going to remember that I'd been patient all day long; the only thing they'd remember was my end-of-day eruption!

As I learned to lower my own personal threshold, I was able to maintain true patience throughout the entire day. My children became accustomed to stricter limits and guidelines, and now my patience does not (often) wear thin.

Think of ways to lower your threshold to stress in other areas of your life. For example, if you're constantly the one at your office who organizes the boss's "surprise" birthday party, or who always volunteers for the last-minute project with the tight deadline, begin letting others take over these non-mandatory tasks. Occasionally it might be *de rigueur* to take on an extra project, but be sure you're not always the one working late. You'll soon realize that much of the added stress was caused by your inability to set limits at work. The idea is to notice your feelings of stress before they have a chance to get out of control. By lowering your threshold at the office, you'll be amazed at how much less stress you'll feel.

What I've learned is that when you have a high threshold for stress, all it produces is more stress. Lower your threshold, and you'll find yourself less reactive and more patient overall, and you and your family will thrive.

37

LET YOUR CHILDREN GROW INTO
THEIR OWN SHOES

When we are given the gift of children, we must remember that a gift is exactly what they are. We are given the opportunity to be responsible for them for a relatively short period in their lives, and to guide them until they are ready to find themselves. Kahlil Gibran states the meaning of this strategy beautifully in *The Prophet* when he says, "As parents, we should allow our children to grow up and become their own people. We should not expect them to be exactly like us."

As parents, it should be our goal to speak to our children as much through our actions as we do with our words. Our children look to us to be their example of how to relate to others and live in the world. They are like sponges absorbing it all, which can be quite a horrifying realization at times! It is important to realize that part of being human is that we are not perfect. Our children learn as much from the mistakes we make in parenting, as they do from making mistakes themselves. It's important to admit to your children when you do make a mistake, so that they can see that everyone is human, and that it's all right to make a mistake if it is sincerely apologized for. Children make such great teachers; they reflect so easily that which they see.

Our youngest daughter, Kenna, has provided us with a unique opportunity to allow her to grow into her own shoes, early on. When she was six years old, she had the realization that meat came from animals that were once alive. Once she became aware of this, she immediately became a vegetarian. Richard and I recognized that this was not an excuse to get out of eating certain foods she didn't like, because before her realization, she was quite the carnivore, devouring hot dogs, steak, and bacon. This was her first true moral decision based on compassion and understanding. She said, "Mommy, I feel the feelings of the animals. I can't eat them." While I wasn't particularly thrilled from a selfish perspective because our family diet was already complicated enough (Jazzy was off wheat and gluten due to an allergy, and meat is one of her only staples; and Kenna wasn't supposed to eat much dairy due to asthma), I knew that I had to support and encourage her. I had to recognize her ability to make a personal and moral choice.

We walk a fine line as parents. If we become over-identified with our children and treat them as possessions, then we find ourselves attempting to place controls on them which are not healthy. It is more healthy to give them boundaries from which they can make the right choices and decisions. Sometimes they will make the choice you would make; sometimes they won't. Just as when they were learning to walk and fell down or bumped their heads, you were there to comfort them, but you couldn't prevent every accident. The same is true as you let your children grow into their own shoes by making choices based on their own value systems.

Another way in which mothers must be careful is not to project their image of themselves onto their daughters. For example, this means not to project your own body image issues onto your daughter, as well as to stay out of the many problems they have with their friends. It is tempting to get caught up in every conflict, especially when there are tears and hurt feelings. Girls always seem to get into their "stuff" early with their friends. It's our job as mothers to empower our daughters with some helpful guidance when asked for it, without making their issues our issues. Remember, too, that there are always two sides to every story and chances are, your daughter is only about 90 percent angel. Experience is sometimes our best teacher; our children learn as much from each other about how to treat people and about developing lasting friendships as they do from watching us.

Richard and I realize that we will face many challenges in our journey as parents. Our measure of success as parents will come in how well we are able to guide our children, but at the same time understanding that many of their choices will be different from the ones we would have made. As adults, they will take with them much of what we have taught them by example, but they will also leave behind what they choose. As separate and independent individuals, they will grow into their own shoes—all sixty-two pairs of them!

38

WRITE A LETTER AND FIND OUT WHERE YOU STAND

Would you like to know where you stand in your relationship with your mother, father, husband, best friend, daughter, son, or sister? If you were going to die tomorrow, what would you say to the most important people in your life? Try this strategy to find out for yourself where you stand in your relationships with the people you care about most. Sit down and write a heartfelt letter.

Don't write this letter with the intention of actually mailing it or giving it to the person. This way, you can write whatever pours out of you without being concerned about how it will be received. Do this exercise when your mind is reflective and quiet.

When you're finished, read the letter, noticing its tone. Were you apologetic? Did you write with a feeling of love and compassion? Were you angry and resentful? Did you thank the person for what they brought to your life? Did you speak of fulfillment or regret?

The greatest part of this strategy is that once you have determined if your relationship is intact or is not, it's not too late to make changes! Live by the standard that if something is in your power to change, go ahead and change it.

If you found yourself apologizing, take this as a cue that you are ready to ask for forgiveness. Don't put off healing a wound in someone you love.

If your tone was grateful, bask in the joy of realizing that your relationship is fulfilling. If it seems appropriate, you might consider sharing your discoveries with this special person. There is nothing better than hearing how much you are loved and the good things you have contributed to another person's life.

If you found anger, resentment, and regret in your letter, ask yourself what small steps you can take today to heal those feelings. Chances are, the other person probably feels the same way. At the end of our lives, we will never regret healing a relationship by reaching out to another person and accepting at least half of the responsibility for bad feelings. As you show a change of heart, the other person will respond to this, even if they don't show it outwardly. You will reap the incredible emotional reward of knowing you did all you could do to heal this relationship.

My worst fear is in looking back on my life and having regrets, especially about the people that I shared my life with. What a gift you can give yourself by making your relationships better before it's too late! Try this strategy and find out where you stand. As you reflect on what you've written, change what you can with the people you care for most. And if you want to, go ahead and send it!

39

GATHER AND LET GO

Women are gatherers by nature. Whether you're a working mom or not, in general, we're the ones who tend to gather food for our families to eat, clothes to wear, and supplies for a variety of family sports and activities. In addition, we gather furniture, dishes, pots and pans, and whatever we need to put our households in order. Some of us take it one step further and gather practically anything we can get our hands on! I consider myself among the best of gatherers; my problem has always been letting go of the old.

There certainly is no trick to bringing things into your house; the strategy, then, is to remember that when you gather something new, to let go of something old. On my trips to Target, Costco, and Walmart, I may come home with ten new things my family may want or need. If I go to one of these stores a week (not including any other shopping I might do) and buy ten non-food items, I will be bringing forty new things into my house each month, and four hundred eighty new things each year! That's a lot of stuff, and that doesn't include any of the gifts that are given on birthdays and Christmas, nor everything everyone else in my family gathers. Our two daughters are already very good "apprentice gatherers." Richard abhors clutter, therefore he leaves 99 percent of the gathering to the women of his household.

We are teaching our children this strategy of letting go, as well. When they go to the mall and pick out a new outfit, they come home and choose something in their closet to give away to someone who can use it. This is absolutely necessary, as we have reached our closet capacity with no more space to spare.

Have you ever noticed that most older houses (like ours) as well as most apartments that aren't new, weren't built with such enormous closets? I think that is because people used to buy just what they needed before the disease of "more" became the focus of our society. Instead of having what we need, we have three in different colors!

Many years ago, people paid cash for the things they bought. The credit card frenzy that took off in the eighties has held a lot of lessons for a lot of people. It taught me what a trap it was to buy something on credit. You can feel like a hamster on a wheel, trying to pay those things off! I'm a pretty low-maintenance partner, if you don't take my Visa bill into consideration! In any case, I have certainly learned my lesson with credit cards.

It's important to develop your own standards for getting rid of the stuff that you don't need. If you are cleaning out your clothes closet, for instance, decide ahead of time and set some ground rules for yourself. If you haven't worn something for six months or since the previous season, toss it into the give-away pile. I like to give my clothes to our local battered women's shelter, where I know that they will be appreciated and well used. It takes less time than trying to sell them on consignment, and it's a good feeling to know you're helping someone who really needs it.

40

STOP SWIMMING UPSTREAM

When I was growing up in the Pacific Northwest, we used to watch the salmon swimming upstream. It was one of the most beautiful and awesome displays of nature I've ever seen. However, unlike the salmon, who must swim upstream to propagate their species, we not only don't need to put out this kind of energy, but in fact, it works against our best interests.

You know you're swimming upstream when you're putting out tremendous effort in some aspect of your life without achieving, or at least heading toward, your desired end result. Swimming upstream means fighting battles we can't win, regardless of our efforts, and even if everything goes as planned! Rather than feeling inspired and satisfied by your efforts, you instead feel incredibly overwhelmed. "I can't do this anymore!", you want to scream.

Arguing is another way that we sometimes choose to swim upstream. It's certainly all right to discuss different points of view—say, in politics—as long as you remain detached from the outcome (that is, if your ultimate goal is to remain peaceful and happy). You may want to keep in mind, however, that there are certain issues, as in religion or politics, where two people may never see eye to eye. Trying to share your experience and expecting agreement with the wrong person can feel a little like discussing quantum physics with a two-year-old. Personally, I would rather listen respectfully, with a detached sense of humor, to someone who has an opposing point of view, than engage in a conversation that makes my blood pressure rise.

Luckily, the tendency to swim upstream is totally reversible. Often, doing so is as easy as having the humility to admit that you're fighting too hard. Humility and recognition of the problem have a calming effect on the spirit, which allows you to consider adjusting your attitude. The next time you feel like you're swimming upstream, consider making some changes that put you in the ebb of a gentler direction. The result will be similar to turning around in the rapids and coasting downstream with ease.

41

DON'T BE A BACKSEAT DRIVER

There are few things more irritating than having someone sit in the backseat of your car, firing off instructions while you're driving. Unless the advice is really needed, as in the case of an emergency or something the driver truly doesn't notice, backseat driving is virtually always unasked for.

Interestingly enough, the same can be said about what you might call "backseat living," meaning someone who is trying to live someone else's life for them or someone who is living their life vicariously through someone else. The classic example of this dynamic is a parent who always wanted to be a great athlete or musician, but wasn't able to make it happen for themselves. So now, as a parent, they push their kids to become accomplished in one of those fields, and they take their pushing to an extreme. Their self-worth is tied up in how well the kids do or don't do.

Backseat living is highly stressful. Not only do you push away and ultimately alienate the people whose lives you are trying to influence, but you also feel incredible amounts of stress and disappointment over things you have no control over. It's hard enough keeping your cool when your own tennis game needs work, but impossible to keep your emotions in check if your sense of well-being is tied to whether your son or daughter happens to win the tournament or whether your boyfriend has the ambition you think he should have!

Being supportive and enthusiastic, of course, are entirely different subjects. I'm referring here to crossing the line into truly unhealthy territory, in which the other person feels pushed and not accepted, and you feel stressed out!

The key to breaking this habit is to first have the humility to admit to yourself that, at times, you practice backseat living. By identifying yourself in that role, you'll be able to take a step back and see the bigger picture. Once you see yourself as a backseat driver (so to speak), the rest is easy—simply turn the tables. Imagine what it would be like to have someone trying to drive your life, always looking over your shoulder, offering unsolicited advice, judging your actions, acting disappointed and disapproving, and so forth. Once you imagine this happening to you, it's pretty easy to see how distasteful it can be. Then you can learn to increase your compassion and back off.

One of the greatest gifts you can offer someone you love is to let them know, in no uncertain terms, that you love them and approve of them, exactly as they are. They don't need to change, or be any different, or take your advice—you simply love them. It's comforting to know that there are people in our lives who have confidence in us, people who show us through their actions that they believe in, and have faith in us.

Life is such a magical gift to be treasured. Perhaps we should allow others to experience this gift without the burden of our backseat driving. To let go of this habit is a gift to those we love, as well as to ourselves.

42

CREATE BEAUTY FROM THE
INSIDE OUT

Have you ever looked at a lively, dynamic woman who radiates energy and light with her charisma and confidence, but when you take stock of her actual features, she's not really beautiful in the traditional sense? However, her beauty is the most magnetic kind, because it comes from the inside out.

The story of the ugly duckling who turns into the beautiful swan always stays close to my heart. The ugly duckling and the swan have always been one and the same. As the duckling matures and grows into herself, she becomes beautiful on the outside as she turns into a majestic swan.

We are no different, as we grow into ourselves and realize who we are on the inside. The transformation that occurs in women who have realized the mind-body-spirit connection is similar to the ugly duckling's transformation. No matter what your physical characteristics, when you are genuinely happy inside and connected to your spirit, you become lit from within with a radiance so fantastic it shines from your very soul.

When magazines and talk shows display the makeovers of women who go from "drab to dazzling," I have always wondered, Why not try a beauty makeover from the inside out, and see if it doesn't have similar results? It's possible that these made-over women look better because they feel better about themselves. Sure, a new haircut and an updated wardrobe looks good, but it also does wonders for your spirit. If you took a woman who was frazzled, insecure, and unhappy, and taught her some tools to help her feel calm, happy, and peaceful, with a more lighthearted attitude, surely she would also become more beautiful!

There isn't a person on earth who is not beautiful while he or she is smiling and experiencing unadulterated joy! True beauty happens from the inside out, and will attract others like a magnet. When you are connected to your own spirit, you know what nourishes you and what doesn't. Like a flower that is beautiful only while it is connected to its life source, every cell in your body experiences the peace you feel inside from this connection, and radiates health. When the flower disconnects from its life source, it withers and dies; and we are no different. Long before we die, we may wither from a lack of connection to our spirit.

Women who are at peace and are happy are also more attractive to their partners. Through this heightened sense of self, such women have developed a greater acceptance of their bodies, which is extremely appealing to most men. Most healthy men are turned off by insecurity, even if the insecure woman looks great. And there is nothing more unattractive, or less sexy, than a woman who may be blessed with outer beauty but who has an ugly attitude!

Cultivating this kind of inner beauty requires some practice and discipline. You must spend some time alone with your self. Women of all ages who meditate and do yoga often appear ageless. They shine with a youthful glow, and their eyes are intensely vibrant.

There are numerous other ways to create beauty from the inside out: A simple time of silence, chanting, or an evening prayer can connect you with your spirit. The discipline is in spending a little time each day in some sort of silence, where the mental chatter is quieted and your mind is stilled.

The truth is, we are all both the ugly duckling and the beautiful swan. As you foster the connection of your mind, body, and spirit, you will radiate the peace and joy you feel inside, and you will become the beautiful swan from the inside out.

43

MY WAY IS NOT *THE* WAY—IT'S
JUST MY WAY

Physically, we are not completely unique or special as women; we're all variations of the same basic stuff. Yet it is the filter through which we see the world and interpret events that sets us apart. In essence, we experience everything not only through our senses, but through the interpretation of our senses. This interpretation comes from our own set of looking glasses, where no two pairs are alike.

Our looking glasses, or interpretation of events, dictates our reality. In a relationship, our interpretations bump up against another's, and at times may collide. In the midst of this collision or conflict, it is helpful to keep in mind the notion that "my way is not *the* way; it's just my way." While you may feel compelled to forge forward in your conflict, understanding and repeating this statement to yourself will give you tremendous compassion as well as humility.

As you say to yourself: "My way is not *the* way; it's just my way," your determination to be "right" at all costs should have a great deal less punch. For instance, look at all the people you are closest to; your spouse, boyfriend, sister or brother, your children, your mother and dad. While much of the time you will see things eye to eye, there will be times you don't, and this is because you each base your view of things on your individual filter system. This can be seen when siblings get together and talk about their mutual upbringing, but have very different stories to tell. You might often wonder how these two people grew up in the same home!

Mary and Susan, who are sisters, have an ongoing dispute about a major parental decision. Mary, who considers herself well-read and an experienced mother of two, believes a family bed (in which childen sleep with their parents at night) is damaging to both the children as well as the spousal relationship. She has read numerous articles that have validated her position and has discussed the issue with friends, pediatricians, and others who agree with her.

Susan vehemently disagrees with her. So much so, in fact, that she believes Mary is not being nurturing and loving enough to her kids. As a mother with a newborn child, she believes that parenting is a twenty-four-hour job and that anyone who disagrees with her position lacks true love and commitment for her children. The articles she has read support her position that *not* to have a family bed is a selfish and damaging act.

Now, who is right? Both have plenty of evidence to support their positions; both love their kids equally; both are great parents. Could the truth be that both are right, from their own perspective?

One thing is certain: If your goal is to create better relationships and live in harmony with others, it's helpful to know, in advance, that while your way may work wonderfully for you, others may see things differently. This more humble way of embracing points of view doesn't diminish your own opinions, but simply enhances your compassion as well as your ability to take conflict less personally.

44

STOP MAGNIFYING THE FLAWS

We can be highly critical and such harsh judges of one another, as if it's a cheap form of entertainment. We call our friend to revel in how our coworker blew it in the meeting. We repeat negative stories. We criticize people for not fitting our perfect images. We look down on people who are overweight or have other physical problems, and in addition, we constantly berate ourselves for not being "perfect." In fact, we wear our perfectionist badge as if it's one of honor. Rarely do we hear people praising each other, and you will not see many front page news articles written on love! Love, it seems, is the scarcest emotion of all in this day and age.

It cracks me up when I'm looking at the pristine features of a newborn baby, and the mother points out her infant's "baby acne." Magnifying the flaws is nothing more than a negative mental habit. And, unfortunately, it is one that's also very contagious.

We need to become aware of when we are thinking critically and holding our magnifying glass too close. As we become less judgmental and we accept that everything is how it was meant to be, we become less critical of ourselves and others, and therefore more happy.

I was in the gym yesterday, and there were two ladies talking while in the bathroom stalls. One said, "Gee, did you see Helen?" The other responded by saying, "Yeah, she got married six months ago; she used to be very pretty." "This might be mean to say, but, yeah, what happened? Maybe that's a good reason not to get married."

I was shocked that these women would have the audacity to make such ugly comments in a public setting. It was the perfect illustration of how we hold others to this measuring stick of perfection while magnifying their flaws. When we make comments and observations of this nature, it speaks more about how we feel about ourselves and our obvious low self-esteem, than of how we see others.

The same can be true when you are overly critical with yourself. I have always been my own worst judge, and can see all too clearly the areas that I need to improve. For instance, instead of focusing on my devotion to my family and all that I do, often I catch myself pining over the areas in which I feel I'm lacking. I have learned that the only place that kind of thinking will get me is down. By catching myself thinking these kinds of thoughts, I can bring my attention back to all that I do, instead of all that I don't do.

Guilt is a familiar emotion to a perfectionist. Say good-bye to magnifying your flaws, and you say good-bye to some unwarranted guilt. There is great freedom in becoming a reformed perfectionist and realizing that "perfection" does not exist in this world!

45

CELEBRATE OUR ABILITY TO
GIVE BIRTH

There are so many aspects to marvel over when contemplating the miracle of birth. Each stage of development takes your breath away: from conception, to hearing the heartbeat of a fetus, to seeing the ultrasound of a child growing inside you, to the passage through the birth canal, and finally snuggling that infant, whole and beautiful, to your breast. There is so much to celebrate!

As women, we are indeed gifted with the incredible task of childbearing. It is the one thing that makes us truly unique, and invaluable to the survival of the human species. Creating a child inside our bodies is a spiritually enriching experience, once we are able to put our fears aside. It is also a process that leaves most fathers in awe of the strength of their female partner, and shows us, as women, just how powerful we are. It is a miracle every time a new person is born on this planet. It's too bad that each time it's not front page news!

Before the birth of our first daughter, Jazzy, I watched a video of a woman giving birth in the traditional way of the Huichole Indians of Mexico. I gained a different perspective about the birthing process, and it helped me to let go of the fear I was feeling, after hearing so many horror stories. This woman on the video made the birthing process a celebration for both the mother and child. This is not a philosophy I would have learned in my Lamaze course!

I watched as this woman went through the birthing process in a natural, homelike setting, surrounded by all the special women in her life. As her contractions peaked in intensity and she got closer to her transition (the latter stage in the birth process), she did not writhe in pain, but rather chanted in celebration that her child was about to arrive. The women around her chanted with her and rubbed her back, helping to prepare her to push. She stood as the infant came through the birth canal, and all the women in the room cheered in jubilation.

This video helped me realize that the birth process is not something to be afraid of. On the contrary, when you begin labor in a relaxed state of mind, trusting that your body knows how to give birth—even if your mind doesn't—you can relax through what many describe as unbearable pain. Of course there will be periods of discomfort and pain in this process, but your ability to maintain the perspective of celebration will help you endure even the most intense moments. As the intensity rises, you are closer to holding that baby in your arms.

I hope that you spend many moments reflecting on your own childbirth experience and marveling in what an amazing gift this ability to give birth really is. Celebrate this with other mothers, and marvel at the miracle of all that your body can accomplish. If you haven't given birth yet, I hope this inspires you to enjoy it when you do eventually get pregnant and have a baby, despite the many scary stories you may hear. And, if you cannot give birth, or have chosen not to, I hope you'll still marvel at the miracle and join in the celebration.

46

LEARN TO MEDITATE AND QUIET YOUR MIND

The quiet mind is our best tool for introspection. As Plato said, "A life unexamined is not a meaningful life." True meaning in life comes through understanding your own nature and learning to accept all aspects of yourself. Through quiet examination, we can begin to create a bridge between our unconscious mind, which we are not completely aware of, and our conscious mind, and reveal to ourselves who we really are on the inside.

If you're unaccustomed to the benefits of meditation, let me share an example that most people can relate to, of a quiet mind. The feeling of the quiet mind is very near to what it feels like when you are entranced by watching a mesmerizing sunset. As the sun goes down and you are ever-present in the moment, you may feel as if time is suspended. The moment seems longer than usual while the sun drops below the horizon. This is similar to the sensation of a quiet mind. In this space, you receive your best creative, reflective, and inspired thoughts. It is what athletes, artists, musicians, and writers alike call "being in the flow." With a quiet mind, you tune in to the moment with full presence.

A quiet mind is an incredible source of creativity. It's as though ideas, solutions, and wisdom are able to percolate and develop. In the absence of the inner "chatter" and noise that is so often present in our minds, our deepest source of wisdom is able to surface. Life seems so much more manageable and so much calmer when the mind is allowed to rest—to settle down and become peaceful.

Other benefits of meditation include emotional stability, as well as a heightened sense of intuition, inner guidance, and a feeling of well-being. When I meditate (for fifteen to thirty minutes every morning), I carry the feeling of quiet with me throughout my day. I am more in tune to my surroundings, better able to listen while other people are talking, less likely to be reactive with my children and husband, and better able to make decisions and to discern priorities. One thing is certain—I sweat the small stuff a whole lot less!

When I meditate, it also feels as if life is far more magical, even though in reality it's exactly the same. Quieting your mind slows down your inner pace, which allows you the presence of mind to experience all that is going on around you with greater awareness and heightened perception.

Meditation is a wonderful tool that will enhance your life tremendously. Meditation creates the bridge to connect the mind, body, and spirit. I encourage you to experiment with a tape, read a book, or better yet, take a class. However you do it, you'll discover the specific type of meditation that's best for you. As you incorporate some form of meditation and/or quieting the mind into your daily schedule, you will experience the peace that comes from being in touch with the very essence of your being. Your life will never be the same!

47

GO AHEAD AND VENT (ONE TIME), BUT GET IT OFF YOUR CHEST

I don't know about you, but when I'm really bugged about something, it's my tendency to vent it—not once, but many times. I'll repeat the same story over and over again. I've even found myself telling one friend—and then another, and another—until I run out of friends to tell! Then I might start again with friend number one, until she gently reminds me that I've told her the story already. Venting becomes a sort of sport, something we do to entertain ourselves, to pass time, and to convince ourselves that we are justified in being annoyed by whatever is bothering us.

It has become clear to me, however, by observing my own feelings and those of others, that such "repeat venting" destroys any potentially positive aspects of the process. Whereas one venting session can be useful, even healing, repetition only bogs you down and stresses you out. Repeat venting serves to feed our hamster wheel mode of thinking, and instead of feeling any sense of relief, we create even more anger and frustration by keeping our stressful thoughts alive. The things that bother us are fed by our attention to them; venting is the perfect way to "stuff" ourselves with our troubles.

Just as we wouldn't intentionally rub salt into an open abscess, if we absolutely must vent (which should be done only to try to gain insight), try doing it with one person, one time, and let it go after that.

There's no question that venting can adversely affect your marriage. Talking about the things that bother you once is fine, but to do so over and over again simply keeps you bothered, and keeps your attention on what is wrong in your life. I've learned that repeated venting is a clear sign that I'm in a low mood, and commiseration with someone else who is also feeling down will surely take you even lower! The most effective way to feel better isn't even more venting, but instead it is to drop these issues and let them rest awhile. Be assured that they will still be there tomorrow if they are real issues, only you'll feel better and will be able to handle them a bit more reasonably.

Go ahead and give yourself permission, one time, to vent to someone else. Get it off your chest, and feel good about doing so. However, try to catch yourself when you go too far. See if you can resist the temptation to stay stuck in negative feelings, which is precisely what happens when you repeatedly vent the same thoughts. I'm guessing that you'll feel a profound difference the very first time you catch yourself and avoid the temptation. Good luck.

48

SET YOUR OWN PRIORITIES

We live in a "gotta keep up, gotta keep going" era. So, do you continue to live like a sheep, just following the flock because of some irrational fear you're not going to keep up? Or do you reflect on the kind of life you really want, and then set your own priorities? My vote is in: Set your own priorities.

Buying in to peer pressure seems ridiculous after the teenage and college years, but many of us buy in without being aware of it. We rarely define what it is that we really want, or ask ourselves the question, "Why do I want this?" We just keep ourselves busy adding more, more, more to our daily routine of too much. We, as mothers, complain of being a chauffeur to our children, and spend countless hours driving them around from activity to activity. Yet we are the ones who fully control the master schedule. How much "quality" family time are we really spending at home?

Much of the time, if we are really honest with ourselves, we are signing our kids up for countless activities and basing many of our priorities on what is going on around us. If our kids aren't doing the same things as everyone else's, we translate this into fearful thoughts such as: "My kids won't measure up. They won't have the same opportunities as other children their age. I'm not a good mother if I don't keep them active."

Really, all we are truly ensuring with this speedy pace is that our children will adopt this philosophy by habit, and you can bet they will do it better. More, more, more running around. They will probably barely remember their childhoods, as it will seem to have been a blur.

What happened to "downtime"? How many kids still run through fields and catch butterflies, press wildflowers, and play with imaginary friends? The answer to the question, "What are your priorities?", is an individual one. Do you want to prioritize blasting around from one sport and dance class to the next, or is one activity per kid, per season enough?

Another thing I've noticed in my own community is the pressure that parents feel to ensure that their children are keeping up with educational standards. I want to know who decided that nowadays, fifth graders have to do the work we did in the seventh grade? The number of hours and degree of difficulty of the homework Jazzy had in fifth grade last year blew my mind. And what shocked me further was the parents who said it was not enough. One day I asked Jazzy, who was ten years old at the time, "Why don't you go outside and play?" She responded in frustration: "Mom, I have too much work today—I can't be a kid anymore!" Boy, don't kids just say it straight the way it is?

While on the one hand, I want my kids to do what is expected of them in school because it teaches them responsibility, I take issue with the amount of work they're being given. As I said in another chapter, childhoods are fleeting, and we only get one chance to create those special memories for our children. I want my kids to grow up and say, "Wasn't being a kid great?"

So, figure out what your priorities really are, and hold on tight to being true to them. You constantly need to ask yourself and your family:

Are we doing too much? Are the activities we are selecting benefiting us—or are they burdening us? Are our children under too much pressure? Are we under too much pressure?

Set your own priorities; evaluate and contemplate the manner in which you are living your life. Live life the way you want to, with your own set of values. Stop running around simply because "you gotta keep up, and you gotta keep going." You will take an enormous weight off your shoulders by letting go of this attitude, and you will find the payoff intrinsically enormous!

49

DON'T TRIP ON YOUR EXCESS
BAGGAGE

We've all been on a vacation where we've packed so much luggage and lugged it around, that it interfered with the quality of our experience. We pack heavy bags and so much stuff that we can't even find what we're looking for. We end up tripping on our excess baggage! Of course, we vow to never do it again. But usually we end up doing the same thing, making the same mistake the next time. Each new vacation brings with it the hope, fear, or fantasy that "This time we really will need it."

Your emotional baggage can drag you down in the same way. That is, unless you see it as "excess," and something you don't have to drag around with you. A dose of humility and some repeated reminders to yourself can go a long way toward ridding yourself of these emotional burdens.

Most of us require a certain amount of material "baggage." For example, you could think of your car as necessary baggage, if you're lucky enough to have one. For many people, myself included, a car is indeed necessary. But along with a car comes the necessary hassles—payments, maintenance, care and cleaning, smog checks, repairs, and all the rest. Most of us wouldn't want ten cars, even if we could afford them—the hassles and time involved would drive us nuts! A lot of "stuff" is like that. A certain amount is great, but too much brings with it more hassle than it's worth. You can end up spending all of your time tending to those things that were supposed to bring you joy—sorting, keeping clean, protecting, replacing, insuring, re-organizing, finding space for, taking care of, and so forth.

There is, of course, necessary emotional baggage, as well. We all come from families, and no family is perfect. We all have limitations and hardships. We all have a personality and a few quirks. Most of us have experienced pain and grief of some kind. We have a set of circumstances and a certain amount of responsibility that we must attend to, no matter what. All of that comes with the territory; no one is exempt.

But then there's the "excess" emotional baggage—things like hanging on to anger or resentments, anticipating or imagining problems that may not even exist, blowing things out of proportion, our tendency to overreact instantly, commiserating too much, focusing on what's wrong instead of what's right, "sweating the small stuff," and so forth. These things, and others like them, push us over the edge, causing us to trip over ourselves. When we carry around the emotional baggage we don't need anymore, we are living in the past.

It's as if we continue to see our life through a cloudy, aged filter; constantly referring to these past moments, expecting our present experiences to be the same. While we are viewing life from a past orientation, we lack perspective and a fresh look at the way things really are. We expect things to be a certain way, and that's all we see.

I believe that most women are remarkably strong and can handle almost anything that comes their way. Yet it's this self-induced stuff, the small stuff that our days are made of, that sometimes gets in our way and makes life too much to handle.

Just as packing a lighter, smaller suitcase is a huge relief when travelling, so too is lightening your emotional load by letting go of any excess baggage you find yourself tripping over. I encourage you to open your emotional suitcase and take a look inside. You may just find a few things you no longer need.

50

PACKING LIGHT AND
TRAVELING RIGHT

Now that we've talked about emotional excess baggage, I thought it would be fun to discuss the literal kind. You've decided to go on a trip for fun! What's not fun is tripping over your excess baggage, in the literal sense, and having a lot more than you need with you. You expend a lot of energy carrying your bags, and it's quite frustrating to realize at the end of your vacation that you didn't wear half of what you lugged around.

I love to travel, but loathe packing. Every time I stand there facing my closet, wondering what I'm going to need and want on this trip. I'll admit that packing light is not my strong suit. In fact, every vacation I go on, I fall one overstuffed bag short of my goal of packing light. I always feel overwhelmed by my options, and wish I could delegate the task to someone else.

So, seeing as though I am no expert on packing light, I thought we'd all get some tips from my good friend, Betty Norrie, who is an agent for the Worth Collection and a women's clothing wardrobe consultant. She is a seasoned traveler who goes light and right at the same time.

Here are Betty's helpful hints to packing light:

- Pack clothing as flat as you can; fill up every corner with a garment.

- Cover every item with, or place every item in a plastic bag from the dry cleaners; nothing will be wrinkled when you arrive at your destination.
- Stuff socks and small things into the corners of your suitcase or into shoes and evening bags; leave your belts long, not rolled, and fit them around the outside edges of the bag.
- To pack a knapsack: Roll items vertically, so you can see them; this way you won't have to repack every time you remove something.
- Tie brightly colored shoelaces to the handles of your luggage to identify it, so no one will take your bag by mistake.

We used a trip to Europe for the following example; however, you could basically pack this way to any city in the U.S. as well. Hawaii, the Bahamas, and other sun-trips require different planning, but you can use these guidelines to help you simplify.

Packing light for a trip to Europe (one to four weeks): Here's what to take:

- One washable, lightweight sleep gown
- Black slacks (2)
- Dark khakis or nice jeans (1)
- White washable tee-tops (2)
- Colored washable tee-tops (2)
- Black easy-to-pack dress (1)
- Black jacket or shawl
- Knee-length or mid-length calf skirt or walking shorts (1)
- A nice blouse or slipover shirt or sweater

- Colorful scarves to accessorize with black clothing (3–4)
- One small, soft, flat black evening bag
- At least one week's supply of undies (you can wash in hotel sinks with a dab of shampoo)
- Stockings and socks
- One dressy black pair of shoes
- Casual black walking shoes (2 pairs)
- If you work out, take one outfit with two T-shirts and one pair of cross-training shoes (wrapped in a plastic bag)
- Simplify your makeup and use travel size for all hair and face products (be sure to pack in separate compartment from clothing to avoid spillage)
- The smallest blow dryer available (don't forget an electric adapter)
- One small soft bag, stuffed in outside pocket of luggage, for souvenirs and mementos

For the airplane:

- Wear a comfortable but nice-looking outfit
- Carry on your coat
- Always keep your valuables in your possession: wallet, passport, credit card, jewelry
- If you can't carry all your bags on, pack one carry-on with a set of clothes in it, just in case your luggage arrives later than you
- Pack a small pouch with everything you would receive in first-class: eye mask, Evian mister spray, ear plugs, extra socks, toothbrush with paste, Chapstick

- Inflatable neck pillow
- A good book
- An extra bottle of water (drink at least one glass per hour)
- Eat one banana—the potassium helps with jet lag

Hints for traveling right:

- Always take a suitcase that has well-tested rollers!
- If you're a coffee drinker, pack your own miniature coffeemaker to avoid astronomical room service bills.
- To best handle time zone changes, immediately get right on the schedule of the country you have traveled to. For instance, if you arrive in Europe in the morning, stay up during daylight hours so you'll be ready for bed when everyone else in that country is.
- Purchase maps of the cities you plan to see before you get there. Blow them up so you can see street corners, and mark your routes out ahead of time.
- Disposable cameras work great for snapshots

We hope these hints make packing more manageable. Have a great trip, without tripping on what you don't need. You surely don't want to be sweating any small stuff while you're on vacation!

GET OFF YOUR HAMSTER WHEEL

It's imperative to avoid getting caught up in your thinking, particularly if you want to experience your low moods gracefully without spiraling even lower. Most of us have mental "tapes" that repeat in our heads over and over; these repetitive thoughts are nothing more than falling prey to a negative mental habit. And, unfortunately and fortunately, our lives are a series of both positive and negative mental habits in living color.

I call this type of mental habit "hamster wheel" or circular thinking. In it, one thought is connected to another thought, and so on; generally, these thoughts follow a remarkably similar pattern. Typically, you have such thoughts when you're discontented or frustrated, and you experience them only while in a low mood.

I'd like to share a most personal example with you. It helped me to understand my own mental dynamic while making the transition from career woman to working mom, and then finally to stay-at-home mom.

It was such a shock bringing our first newborn infant home from the hospital! I had no idea how consuming the responsibility of parenthood would be, and the devotion it took to be a nursing mom. I had previously worked very diligently in my graphic design business, and was devoted to its success. However, there was no comparison to the daily and nightly responsibilities of motherhood. At one point when I was pregnant with Jazzy, I actually had had an image of her going to work with me and lying happily in a playpen while I continued to work. "Happily" was the operating factor that I later realized was my illusion; ignorance truly can be bliss.

It was quite a transition to get used to my sporadic work schedule, which now included day care, and I was in no way equipped to handle the cling-on infant that was my first daughter. She must have had an instinct that told her to hang on for dear life, because that is exactly what she did. My previously independent nature bumped directly up against a 100 percent dependent infant. I almost went nuts on numerous occasions, as there were brief periods when she barely tolerated even Richard caring for her.

During this time, I realized that my thoughts would follow a certain pattern as I contemplated a solution to balancing work with motherhood. If I was fatigued (which of course, being sleep-deprived, I was), then I would become depressed. My thoughts kept circling around how I was ever going to manage my client base and uphold the same standards for my work—which had been previously all-consuming—and find time to raise a child. I would spiral even lower.

Luckily, after about ten thousand runs on this identical hamster wheel of thought, I had an insight, and I finally stepped off. I simply noticed the train of thought I would get into when I was tired and low. I learned to say something like this to myself: "Oh! There you go again. You don't want to go there, girl." And I'd manage to stop myself. It was one of the simplest insights I'd ever had, but clearly one of the most powerful.

After all, what comes first, the thought or the feeling? The thought comes first, of course, as our minds are constantly on the go. As long as we are breathing, we are thinking creatures too. It is impossible to feel low without first having low thoughts, or frazzled without having frazzled thoughts. At times, it may seem that the opposite is true. But this is only true because we forget that we're thinking—and we forget the impact our thinking has on the way we are feeling. If you'd like, try it for yourself. Try to get mad or stressed—right now—without thinking about something that makes you mad or stressed!

I illustrate this concept to my children when they are worrying about something that hasn't happened yet. I'll say: "Think of an ice cream cone. When you think of the ice cream cone, does it appear right in front of you just because you're thinking about it?" Of course, they realize it does not. Your thoughts are as imaginary as the ice cream cone; just because you think them, it does not mean that they are real. Knowing this allows you to see your thoughts merely as thoughts, thereby taking them a little less seriously.

52

USE YOUR CAREER FOR YOUR
SPIRITUAL WORK

Let's face it, we spend more time working than we do anything else. If you wait until Sunday to practice your spirituality, you are missing out on the greatest opportunity for spiritual growth, and you'll probably be too tired to make much of an impact anyway. Much of spirituality is about nourishing your own spirit, as well as nurturing others through finding everyday ways to serve. You can do this simply by going about your work and living by your spiritual principles and values.

You don't have to be Mother Teresa or the Dalai Lama to use your career as your spiritual work. It really doesn't matter what line of work you're in; whatever you do provides interaction with other people, and wherever there are people, there will be spiritual opportunity. Your spirit can connect with another's, and you can nourish each other. We are all teachers and counselors; the key is to incorporate your spirit into your everyday interactions. It is, after all, not what you do, but how you live your life that will constitute your ultimate impact on the world. As Gandhi said, "Your life is your message," and it won't matter much what title appears on your business card.

When you find yourself in a sticky situation with a coworker, you can choose to resolve the situation with love and compassion. There are, of course, situations that arise in which you must hold people accountable for their actions. This is also a spiritual opportunity. The way you choose to deliver the lesson reveals how you incorporate your spirituality. You want the person to learn about their own nature in the process of the interaction. If you need to terminate someone's employment, do you do it from a place of love and compassion? Your actions and the feelings behind them speak to your ability to do your work in combination with spiritual energy.

There is a great quote that my neighbor shared with me, that speaks to the heart of this strategy: "The divine in you meets the divine in me to form a better understanding." Keep this in mind as you deal with conflict, and you will be better able to keep things in perspective.

I met a woman recently through some rather unfortunate circumstances. My first and treasured horse, Shasta, had reached an old age where her quality of life was nonexistent. I had to come to the decision that it was better for her to die peacefully, as opposed to constantly falling down and suffering. I had delayed having her put to sleep for some time, but even so, making those arrangements was very difficult for me. I had to call the vet as well as a livestock disposal service. The vet was easier than the latter. Ugly thoughts about what they would do with her body kept occurring to me.

Finally, I called the name on the card and talked to a very nice woman who helped to reassure me that I was doing the right thing. Yet it wasn't until I met her the next morning that I was fully reassured that I could trust my treasured pet with this person. The woman who showed up with her big truck walked to me with her arms opened wide, and I felt the compassionate and caring presence of a hospice healer. The look in her eyes was so comforting that I knew that as hard as her job was, it was her spiritual work. She helped me, a complete stranger, follow through with peace in my heart as I was enveloped in her warmth and loving feeling. I was a person in need emotionally, a complete stranger to her, and she was there to help me with loving support.

Whether you're a businessperson, a hospice worker, a mother, or a grocery clerk, use your career as your spiritual work by incorporating your spirit in all you do. Use the talents and gifts that the Creator has given you to give back to others through your work, and it won't matter what you do; you will find fulfillment.

You may ask yourself: Do you reach out when someone is in need? Are you able to get beyond first impressions and see what's under a person's insecurity? Can you see the innocence in people's actions? Are you able to hold people accountable with love and compassion?

As you incorporate your spirit into your work, all the while nurturing those around you, you will get more satisfaction from your career than you ever imagined possible.

53

KNOW WHEN YOUR EGO IS
GETTING THE BEST OF YOU

Recently, while on a meditation-yoga retreat, I took a course that described the ego in the best way I had ever heard or read. I was taught that we have two parts to our identity: our great "self," which is our true spirit, and the smaller self, which is our ego.

The ego holds us at bay from communicating and being in touch with our true self; that is, who we really are on the inside. It's as if we are two people: the kind, generous, gentle and loving one, who has access to wisdom and health; and the other, who is vain, greedy, impatient, void of compassion and understanding, and sometimes downright hostile.

These are the two voices that we hear in our heads. At times, it can feel as though these two, the true self and the ego, do battle with one another. In some cases, the ego is in charge so much of the time, the true self is hidden; therefore, the person feels empty and miserable except when the ego is temporarily gratified. The key to true contentment is to know when your ego is getting the best of you.

It was never clear to me, until recently, exactly when I was in my ego state of mind versus when I was in my true self, which is genuinely my own true nature. Now, I have an easy way to tell which one is speaking. It's quite simple: the ego urges you to define yourself. It says, "I am a something. I am a mother. I am an author. I am intelligent," and so on and so forth. The true self says only, "I am," and needs nothing attached to that. "I am," while fulfilling my responsibilities as a mother. "I am," while loving my children from an unconditional place in my heart. "I am," while writing this book. I am myself, which is undefined by my resumé, physical characteristics, personality, or anything else, for that matter.

You can still be intent upon resolving your issues while allowing your true self to speak. You just don't go about it in the same way that you do when you're coming from your ego. Your communication has less bite, and is gentler and more compromising. You don't have to be a pushover; but you don't have to act like a child throwing a tantrum, either.

When you begin to feel the difference between being in your ego versus being in your greater self, you realize how liberating it is to hold your ego at bay. Your inspiration and peace of mind soars as you connect with who you truly are on the inside. The ego muddles you with never-ending desires and illusions, and can never be satisfied. If you're in pain, chances are, you're in your ego state of mind. As you learn to identify when your ego is getting the best of you, you will free your true self, which is best qualified to run your life and to make you happy.

54

STAY OPEN TO MEETING
A NEW FRIEND

After we marry, or are in a long-term relationship, our husbands or partners and children tend to dominate our time, and any other free time is usually spent with old friends and family. As our current acquaintances and friendships fill up our lives, it is tempting to shut ourselves off to new relationships. However, there are several good reasons for staying open to meeting a new friend.

You never know when you're going to meet someone with whom you feel a kindred spirit. He or she may well turn out to be one of those people who help to nourish your spirit most. We've all had the experience of meeting someone who, from the very first, we feel we have known our entire lives. While it is a rare and unique connection, it is one that you don't want to miss simply because you feel too busy to embrace a new person in your life.

We are all here to help guide and learn from each other. Perhaps we have a spiritual pact with certain individuals to help each other along on the path of life. I know that I feel instrumental to many of my friendships, and in the same way, I know there are those friends and special people in my own life who have helped to guide me, as well. I am not a believer in "chance" meetings or luck. We all find each other because of a deeper purpose and our divine connections to one another. Whether it be soul mate or soul sister, you must stay open to embracing these special people as you meet them.

I met one of my dearest friends, my running partner, by what on the surface appeared to be an accident. We saw each other at a gate entrance to a park. Both smiling, both running alone, it was just a natural thing to jog together. Four years later, we have been running together since that first meeting. People ask me how I have the discipline to maintain my fitness, and I have one word to say—Carole. She is a great fitness inspiration as well as a great listener; we spend at least five hours together each week, talking, venting, and laughing. We do a lot of laughing, sometimes so much we can't breathe.

We must treat our friends like gold, since friendship makes our path pleasurable and our experience richer. So stay open to a new friend, no matter how busy you are—the blessings are infinite. We have an abundance of love to give, and our friendships are the place to begin.

55

AGE GRACEFULLY

Aging gracefully is definitely a challenge, given our youth-oriented culture. All of our advertising screams "Youth!," and buying into this message can be a degrading process if you don't adopt an opposing mindset.

While interviewing several women whom I respect for aging gracefully, I asked them what it is about their attitude and lifestyle that has helped them to age with grace. I discovered several consistencies in what they said. Taking care of their physical health was the obvious constant; they eat right, drink lots of water, and get plenty of exercise and rest, and of course, use sunblock. The message I gleaned was: when you have your health, you feel and look good.

Another similarity among these women had to do with the mind-body-spirit connection. We need to nurture, feed, and cleanse our spirits in the same way we care for our appearance and physical health. As we do so, we not only improve our appearance, but we feel younger, as well. Women who age with the most grace have found some kind of peaceful silence in their lives. While they are incredibly active, they also value their time alone. They find an individual path to nurturing their spirit through prayer, meditation, yoga, church, art, gardening, or some other "path." Each person must find her own way, and as she does so, it shows in her peace of spirit.

These women also feel at peace with their age. They aren't stressed about trying to look younger; instead, they are the best they can be for the age that they are. They maintain an attitude that is optimistic, energetic, and adventuresome. The women who keep their spirit of adventure alive, no matter what their age, seem to age with the least resistance. The old saying, "You are only as young as you feel," gains real meaning at the fifty-plus stage of life. I have seen grandmothers do cartwheels with their grandchildren and jump waves in the ocean like schoolgirls; their zest for life makes them shine. A playfulness of spirit and a lack of seriousness enhances their vitality.

As I enter midlife, I have realized that, as women, we need to accept the changes that occur in our bodies and faces. I used to freak out when I noticed my smile lines becoming crevices, and crow's-feet spreading like spiders around my eyes. I have been blessed, however, with knowing many women, including my own mother and aunts, who have felt better about themselves as they aged than they did when they were young. I remember asking my mom, when she was in her forties, how her attitude remained so positive about aging. She said that it was simple for her; she felt in better shape now than she did in her twenties, so she had nothing to feel bad about. I remember admiring her point of view, and hoping that I would feel the same way some day.

As we get older, our metabolisms shift and our hips change shape. We can defy some of these changes with diet, exercise, and weight maintenance, but at some point, we must accept our body's changes as a fact of life and see the beauty in all its various stages. We are different at every age, and beautiful too. Thank God—how boring to stay exactly the same for our whole lives! A friend of mine in her fifties said she has finally come to the place where she can love her cellulite and see the beauty in that too. (That's real progress in my book!)

56

CONSIDER THAT HE MAY NOT HAVE THE "EYE" FOR IT

Have you ever thought about how ridiculous it would be to get frustrated at a person who was blind because she could not see? Or, how pointless it would be to become angry at a child because he could not tell time or drive a car? I've learned that there are times when it's equally pointless to get stressed at grown men over certain things because, the truth is, they simply don't have the eye for it.

I've known many men, for example, who don't have the eye for something to be really neat and clean. I've known others who could define the word "organized," but wouldn't have the slightest capacity to *be* organized.

My father is one of those guys who can fix or put together virtually anything. So, as I was growing up, "fix it" things were never an issue. If something broke, my dad could repair it. Richard, on the other hand, would be the first to tell you he doesn't have the eye (or the hands) for fixing things. Only with great strife can he put those "easy to assemble" purchases together. After what seemed like hours, and a great deal of frustration, he once put our first crib together, and proudly carried it to the nursery. He stood in the doorway, only to find out that it wouldn't fit through the door. Poor man! Whether it has to do with something electrical, the plumbing, or putting something together for the kids, he invariably gives up and tries to find someone to help him. For me to become upset with him would be counterproductive and pointless. It's not intentional, and it's not like he doesn't try—he just can't do it! I've learned to appreciate him for his talents, and realize that in this one particular way, I certainly didn't marry my father.

I've known many women who are frustrated about something their boyfriend or husband can't do. But if you think about it, what's the point of becoming bothered when, in reality, they simply aren't able?

Some people don't have the knack for being on time. Others can barely boil water. Perhaps there are things you don't have the eye for—being clutter-free, investment strategizing, interior decorating, or whatever. Would you want someone furious or frustrated at you because you have certain strengths and weaknesses? Or, would you prefer that they give you a break and love you just the way you are?

Don't get me wrong. This isn't to say that you allow anyone, men or women, to walk all over you or take advantage of you. Neither is it to say that you don't bring up issues or discuss your preferences. Rather, it's simply to say that, in the end, it's important to choose your battles wisely. If you're frustrated by something the man in your life is doing—or isn't doing—it's often best to focus your attention on those areas where change is at least possible. Unless it's a critical or truly serious issue, or unless it's something that's really driving you crazy, the best strategy is to make allowances for the fact that there are things he's simply not good at.

Simple as it seems, this recognition pays huge dividends in the quality of your life. Rather than spending your time and energy fussing over things that aren't likely to change and over which you have little or no control, you'll shrug off your frustrations and become a bit more lighthearted. So if he doesn't have the eye for something, let it go. Your energy is better spent on other things. And if he tries to do something he doesn't have the eye for, smile with appreciation but keep your chuckles to yourself!

57

GO INSIDE FOR THE ANSWERS

All people are born with innate health. This means that there is an intelligence inside all of us, in the beginning of our lives, that is purely wise and uncontaminated by negative mental conditioning. In time, however, each of us learns, creates, and ultimately practices certain mental habits that prohibit us from accessing this inspirational and creative wisdom.

By engaging in these habits, which are usually invisible to us, over and over again, we learn to focus our attention on the stimuli of the outside world. This distracts us from the emotional pain and suffering we feel inside. Ironically, it is the emotional separation from our spirit that causes us all the pain and suffering to begin with—so this is one of those well-intended unconscious strategies that simply doesn't work.

By now I'll bet you're asking: "How do you go inside?" Going inside only requires two elements: yourself and quiet. You must find your own path to quietness: it could be through prayer or meditation, or enjoying nature, yoga, running, gardening, mountain climbing, or riding a horse— any way that you find time to connect with your spirit, which is like a flame burning inside you, waiting to be refueled. Going inside involves the emptying of your mind; the clearing of your head. Just as you fill up your mind with plans, goals, dreams and disappointments, the opposite is true when connecting with your inner self—you empty your mind of the ongoing chatter and noise. And when your mind is clear, your inner intelligence kicks in and automatically takes over. Decisions, responsibilities, and all aspects of life become easier. You've tapped into the moment.

As you learn to respect the value of a quiet mind and place your attention on the moment, you nurture your ability to be present-moment-oriented, free from your worries, concerns, and inner tribulations; all those things that eventually turn into insecurity and self-destructive or erratic behavior.

As a result, you will feel more connected to everything and everyone who shows up in your life. You will heal, as well as be a healer. As you quiet your mind, you'll begin to slow down and make more balanced decisions. As you practice living from the inside, you are less confused about your life's direction and more peaceful, patient and loving in your relationships. You will have more compassion and understanding, and an enhanced ability to communicate through the love in your heart.

Today, we see all kinds of charismatic, successful, and intelligent people of all ages, who are staved spiritually. They may have mastered the challenges of the outside world by becoming experts in their respective fields, yet their inner spirit is starving for nourishment. Therefore they find themselves unhappy and miserable, despite the fact that they may have accomplished many of their goals and dreams.

Separation from our spirit causes us so much anxiety and depression. We develop coping mechanisms that temporarily pacify our internal longing. Any addiction is only a symptom of your lack of connection to your innate health and spirit. Once you go inside, however, and reconnect, you'll realize that this spirit is the source of your deeper, positive feelings.

It's also where you grow personally, and this growth is what your soul will take with you beyond this world.

The beauty of our humanness is that we can search for meaning from the inside out and rework our individual tapestry, one thread and one habit at a time. As we find our spirit and learn to nurture that connection, we heal.

As you go inside for the answers, what you need to do to reconnect with your inner spirit will become clear. You will begin to experience real and lasting joy as well as peace of mind, and the greatest benefit of all is that you can enjoy the outside world and all it has to offer as a complement to your inner experience.

58

DRESS FROM THE INSIDE OUT

I love clothing as much as the next gal, and find that dressing can become something to look forward to as part of a daily adventure. It gives me one more avenue (albeit one of those fun, yet somewhat superficial ways) to go inside and get to know myself. I've learned that there is no need to struggle every day with the decision of what to wear—instead, we can learn to dress from the inside out.

The idea is to close your eyes and contemplate what you are feeling on any given day. Try dressing yourself intuitively, and express yourself each day by making sure your choice coincides with your mood.

Before going to your closet, close your eyes and ask yourself, "What kind of mood am I in today?" Ask yourself the question, "What color and style will express how I am feeling?" There are, of course, many days when we are limited to wearing what is appropriate to our daily activities, and not necessarily what we would choose based on how we feel. For instance, although you might feel like wearing your evening dress with spaghetti straps during the day, you might consider saving it for the right occasion, unless you truly want to make a "statement" of some sort and turn some heads! You may want to try a black suit and silk scarf instead.

The beauty of people is that, like flowers, we come in all shapes, sizes, and colors. No matter what you look like or what you weigh, you can choose a unique style (or several) that fits you like a glove. Dressing can be such a fun and imaginative way to express your personality.

When you're feeling good, you tend to shine. Pick one of these days to look in the mirror and notice the good stuff about yourself. Go ahead and compliment yourself; it doesn't hurt much!

Find your unique style, and enjoy yourself a bit! Remember that you are dressing to express what is inside you. By doing this, you'll get to love who you are, and your confidence will soar!

59

USE SYMBOLS TO REMIND YOU OF YOUR SPIRIT

One way to merge the material with the spiritual is to create symbols that remind you of your spirituality. For centuries, religions have done this very thing by creating temples and churches with ornate and symbolic architecture and designs. Egyptian as well as Greek cultures worshipped their idols and gods, revering their sculpted images in stone.

Some friends of ours set a beautiful example of how you can use the material world to symbolize and remind you daily of your spirit. They were attending a marriage retreat to renew the strength of their spiritual union. On a blackboard, the leader drew a blue heart to symbolize a point he was making about communicating at the heart level. He had chosen blue chalk arbitrarily to illustrate his example, but the concept spoke so clearly to this couple they decided to make the blue heart their spiritual symbol. They have many symbols, from a blue heart crystal pendant to discreet blue heart tattoos, to remind them of their mutually shared insight and special time together.

Garden spaces are a beautiful way to create a spiritual place in your home where you can foster peace and serenity. Placing stones with inscriptions like "harmony," "peace," "kindness," "patience," and "love" are a great way to remind yourself of these ideals, and what better place to contemplate them but on your morning or evening ritual of sitting in the garden?

You could find a corner in a closet or room to devote to your spiritual symbols. For example, we have a three-tiered stand with glass shelves which holds our crystals, drawings, and pottery the kids make, as well as reminders of our spiritual teachers. It takes very little room, and blends right into our decor. This corner serves as a place designated for prayer, meditation, and yoga, and helps us to integrate our spiritual practices into our daily activities.

You may want to collect physical reminders of the spiritual moments you experience on your travels. These don't have to be trips to a monastery or retreat; if you have an hour of inner peace while hiking on a mountain trail, you might save a small stone as a reminder of that wonderful feeling. Or if you make a trip to the beach and take a quiet, introspective walk under the stars, you might want to take home a seashell to remind yourself of your thoughts during that walk. I recently spoke with a person who had just arrived home from a Caribbean cruise with tremendous peace of mind. He said that he found it challenging to maintain this feeling, but he did want to try. So, he listens to Caribbean music as a reminder of how relaxed he was while on his trip.

Merging the material and spiritual worlds is one of our challenges as human beings. But once you become aware of these simple ways in which to remind yourself of your spirituality, you may find that they can help you to make the connection between the outer world and your rich inner life.

60

REMAIN CALM AND MAKE THE
BEST OF A BAD SITUATION

Whether it's financial worry, a delayed flight, or a coworker we just don't like, there are times we all find ourselves in a spot we would rather not be in. While this strategy is somewhat clichéd, it will hopefully serve as a reminder to you that in every situation, you can choose which path you will take and how you will respond. You can either become enraged and fight back, or surrender calmly, when appropriate, and make the best of the situation.

An example most people can relate to is when a flight is delayed or canceled at the airport. You are tired and ready to return home, and are probably at the end of your fuse anyway. When there are one hundred fifty other people who have no control over their departure time, airplanes are not the only things you'll find flying around at airports! Most people become enraged and take their frustrations out on the ticket clerks, as if they could possibly do anything about it. Very few will make the best of a bad situation.

Just to illustrate what can happen when you are one of the ones to keep your cool, I was once bumped up from coach to first class because I was the only person who stayed calm when my flight was canceled. I decided that my frustration over the situation would do nothing but compound the emotions around me, and frazzling the attendant at the counter was surely not going to get me home sooner. I decided that with two small children waiting at home, and rarely having the chance to read, I would use the time as an opportunity to finish my book. The attendant noticed my patience and rewarded me with a first-class ticket when I got in line to board.

You may find yourself working with someone with whom you have a personality conflict. You can make yourself and all your colleagues miserable, or you can choose to put your differences aside and turn this communication barrier into a spiritual lesson. The philosopher Gurdjieff points out that it is the people who irritate us the most and whom we find most challenging to be around that become our best spiritual teachers. This is because you can look at what is bothering you about another human being and turn it into an opportunity to become more introspective, as well as more compassionate and understanding of your fellow beings.

The next time you find yourself in a sticky situation (which is probably going to be today or tomorrow), I hope you remember that you do have a choice in how you handle it. You can make the choice to remain calm; everyone around you will benefit, and you can rest assured that you are doing your part to create peace for yourself and others. If you do, you are definitely choosing not to sweat the small stuff!

61

RISE ABOVE THE RUT
OF YOUR ROUTINE

Bake bread on Monday. Marketing on Tuesday. Laundry on Wednesday . . . etc. Many people find a routine comforting, as it gives them some feelings of control in life. What can sneak up on us and catch us unaware, however, is an emotional rut that leaves us feeling empty and uninspired. If you are having these feelings, consider finding a time either weekly or daily to expand your horizons a bit and make a minor shift in your routine. A fresher outlook will help you to rise above your rut and the feelings that go with it.

The first step in rising above the rut of your routine is to spend some quiet time reflecting and dreaming a bit. Notice what pops up in your head: it may be something you've been longing to do, but simply have continued to put off. This is the first baby step in learning to live from the source of your inspiration as opposed to staying in the gridlock of your routine.

Some people are a bit structure-stiff. They never deviate from their day-to-day routine, which makes them feel safe. These people can lack fresh inspiration, look more tired and older every year, and never appear to feel enriched or excited about living. While there are certainly parts of our routines such as school schedules, athletic practices, and work schedules that are rarely negotiable, you can sometimes find some small chunks of time that may be.

Consider learning a new language; dare to dream of visiting that country and getting to know the people there. Take an art class. Join a book club, or better yet, start one. Join a church, temple, or other spiritual center. Take up yoga. Alter your exercise routine. There are hundreds of possibilities.

It also does wonders to try to make spontaneous plans, at least every once in a while. I know this becomes more difficult once you have a family with schedules to plan around, but go ahead and find a negotiable slot in your week and do something different. It might be as simple as forgoing the kids' normal homework time for a family nature walk instead. Or, call some neighbors on Sunday morning and invite them over for a barbecue that evening. Give yourself the joy of doing something unplanned or different. It can shake you up and inspire a fresh perspective on life.

Another way to make a simple shift in your routine is by altering your normal driving routes. You might take the more scenic back roads home from work now and then, instead of always getting on the freeway. Driving can be a pleasure if you're not always on the same routes. Also, as you alter your route, consider that it may even be safer for you and your family as it may keep you more attentive and alert. Taking the same route all the time tends to make us daydream.

It is amazing how making one slight shift, in what seems an insignificant gesture, can inspire and uplift your spirit. This feeling will spill over into other areas of your life as you send your unconscious mind the message that you are open to new possibilities. It also, very simply stated, makes life a little less bland and a lot more original.

62

BE GRATEFUL FOR SMALL THINGS

It seems that, often, we become immune to and much less grateful for the small things in our lives. We allow our feelings of being overwhelmed and our yearning for achievement and material satisfaction to overshadow the precious little gems of life that are all around us. In our quest to experience the more seductive and exciting big "highs," we have lost sight of the fact that most of life, indeed a vast majority of it, is made up of small things and small moments, one right after the other.

Learning to appreciate these things and moments plays a huge role in creating a peaceful and happy life. Although the things themselves may be small, failing to appreciate them has some really big ramifications! The failure to acknowledge and, indeed, appreciate the small things means an inability to be touched by life. Rather than seeing and experiencing the perfection of God's plan, most of it is instead disregarded. The wonder and awe of life is diminished, the feelings associated with appreciation and gratitude are missed, and, perhaps more than anything else, you'll be sweating the small stuff big time. The reason this happens is that, when your attention isn't on what's right, beautiful, special, and mysterious, it will be on what's wrong, what's irritating, and what's missing. Your focus of attention will encourage you to be "on edge" and on the lookout for problems.

Unfortunately, this type of attention feeds on itself and becomes a way of seeing and experiencing the world. You'll be too busy thinking about the condescending remark you overheard at lunch or the way your blouse doesn't look quite right to notice the friendly smile of the checkout clerk or the beautiful art on the classroom wall.

On the other hand, when the bulk of your attention is on what's right with your life, what's precious and special, the payoff is enormous. You'll re-experience the feeling that life is magical and to be treasured. Instead of complaining about the litter on the side of the road, you'll notice the colors of the trees and plants. Again, your attention will feed on itself and, over time, you'll notice more and more things to be grateful for. Your habit becomes a self-fulfilling prophecy.

When you talk to anyone who is very sick or who has had a near-death experience, they will tell you that the things you usually think are "big" are, in fact, relatively insignificant; whereas the things you think of as small are, in fact, what's most important. Money, for example, or physical beauty, or an accomplishment or a material possession, can seem to be the end-all, extremely important, sometimes even life-and-death issues. Yet, when looking back on your life, it's very likely that these things will seem to have lost their luster. They will seem less important, maybe even superficial. On the other hand, the beauty of nature, the touch of a newborn, a lovely smile, or the gift of friendship, will seem precious. Indeed, if you knew that you had only one day to live, what would you think about—your car or favorite pair of shoes, or would it be the more everyday joys that would occupy your mind?

A person who celebrates only the big stuff and "highs" will have only fleeting moments of happiness, at best. On the other hand, a person who feels grateful for the small things in life will be happy a majority of the time. Virtually everywhere she looks, she will find cause for celebration.

This isn't a prescription to pretend that things are better than they are, or a suggestion that there isn't plenty of ugliness and pain in the world—there is. What it is, however, is the acknowledgment that, when you are honest and reflective about what's most important in life, it's the smaller things that win the prize.

63

HONOR YOUR MOTHER

There's really nothing more healing and gratifying than honoring the two people—your mother and your father—who gave you the gift of life. Your mother, however, was the vessel that allowed for your arrival, and the first role model in your life as a woman. Since this is a book for women, let's devote a few minutes to her.

The act of honoring your mother is symbolic of an even more important issue. The idea is to reflect upon people in your life, like your mother, who have sacrificed on your behalf simply because they love you. Whatever your current relationship, you need only one reason to honor your mother and be grateful to her, and that is merely because you are sitting here, right now. Without her, you wouldn't exist—not in the same way you do today, anyway!

There are few things that we can utterly, without question, know for a fact to be true, and one of them is that each of us inhabiting the earth got here through our mother. If your birth mom is not the one who raised you, certainly you should, of course, honor the one who nurtured you.

Most people will not have had "perfect" parents (if there is such a thing!). Over the years, your relationship with your mother has in all likelihood had its ups and downs. I'm sure that you haven't seen eye to eye on all things, but you're probably more like her than you care to admit sometimes. If you're like me at all, your appreciation went up one hundred-fold after you became a mother yourself. We can't really know the depth of that commitment and what it really means to be a mother until we are one.

After giving birth to our first daughter, Jazzy, I finally understood the depth of my own mother's loyalty, love, and selfless commitment that she gave to my brother and me.

There are many ways you can honor your mother; the obvious and very least is with a well-wishing phone call or card on Mother's Day or on other special occasions. Yet sometimes an unexpected visit or call just to say, "Hello, how's your day going? By the way, I love you," is a great way to honor her. In addition, there are few things better than a heartfelt letter that arrives unprompted by obligation, and that reads something like:

> *Dear Mom,*
> *I just wanted to say thanks for bringing me into this world; I appreciate the sacrifices you made to make me. I want you to know that, to me, you are a treasure purer than any amount of gold, and I honor you for giving me my gift of life.*
> *Love, your daughter*

Can you imagine how nice it would be if every daughter, everywhere in the world, would write and send a note like this to their own mother?

64

CELEBRATE BEING SINGLE!

I recently heard Marlo Thomas say in an interview, "I wish someone would have told me that, just because I'm a girl, I don't have
to get married!" Her comments inspired me to include "Celebrate being
single" in this book.

I know it's been a while since I was single, so a critic who feels it's
much harder to be single than ever before, or who's convinced that marriage is the only worthwhile goal, might think, "Easy for her to say."
Nevertheless, I've known and met so many people who do indeed genuinely celebrate being single, that I felt it would be an appropriate strategy
to include in the mix.

From a spiritual point of view, we all face the challenge of being
happy. We usually do one of two things: We're either grateful, celebrating
the life we have, or we're busy wishing it were different. After all, the
greatest source of unhappiness for each of us—single, married, divorced,
seeking, widowed, whatever—is the same: Whenever we wish or demand
that things are different from the way they are, we suffer emotionally.
The harder we wish, the more we suffer. There are no exceptions to this
rule. Conversely, the more we embrace what actually is (e.g., our actual
life circumstances) instead of what we wish would be or could be, the

more content we will be. As you probably already know, contentment tends to produce further contentment.

A person who is married but yearns to be single will suffer in the same way that a person who is single, but yearns to be married or in a committed relationship. It's that gap between where you are and where you want to be that creates the pain. If you narrow the gap, you lessen the pain.

Believe it or not, the simple acknowledgment of this dynamic can lead to a world of insight. In other words, awareness of what is actually causing one's pain can be the ultimate prescription to get rid of it. Most important, this recognition opens the door to experiencing and, yes, even celebrating the tremendous advantages of being single.

Anyone can create a list of the obvious advantages of being single—various forms of freedom, diversity, less compromise, the ability to make your own decisions, to name just a few. But none of it means anything beyond a superficial pep talk, without the spiritual insight to support it. That's why it's so important to become aware of the inner dynamics that create pain; the tendency to wish things were different. In the absence of these thoughts, your heart and mind will open to new possibilities. In other words, you'll not only be able to list the advantages of being single—you'll actually embrace, celebrate, and take advantage of them, as well!

Pamela spent her entire adult lifetime yearning to be married. It was so important to her that she (along with some help from her parents and some friends) had convinced herself she couldn't be happy being single. Her desperation showed up in most of her relationships and she was, in fact, miserable. She had linked being single to unhappiness in the same way you might link touching a hot iron to burning your hand.

However, at some point in her life, she began to investigate the world of inner peace. She learned to meditate, spent time at a spiritual center, and became more reflective. She began to recognize the connection between her own thoughts and beliefs and her own level of happiness (and unhappiness). Over time, she began to open her heart to the life she already had. As those familiar thoughts of disappointment and heartache entered her mind, she paid less attention to them and pushed them away. For the first time, she embraced her life, the way it actually was.

What happened to Pamela was quite miraculous. She saw, for the first time, some tremendous advantages of being single. She started doing things that many of her married friends weren't able to do. She traveled and became more friendly to others. She took some interesting classes. She dated more men, not in an attempt to find a husband, but simply for the fun of it. In short, she began celebrating the gift of being single. In a matter of time, she was happier than she ever imagined she could be. She had learned to love being single. Whether or not she ever chooses to be married is irrelevant. If she does, she'll know how to be happy in that situation, as well.

Being single is no better or worse than being married. It's simply a different set of circumstances, complete with different advantages and disadvantages. Like every other aspect of life, there are trade-offs. The mistake so many people seem to make—single or married—is that they remember and focus on the disadvantages, but fail to celebrate the upside.

I once heard of a couple who asked a spiritual advisor whether or not he felt they should get married. At the time, his answer surprised me. Today I understand exactly what he meant. He told the couple, "It doesn't really matter. Remaining single will lead to one set of circumstances, and being married will lead to another set of circumstances." He wasn't being sarcastic, nor was he advocating marriage or non-marriage. He was simply pointing out the reality of the choices we make.

I know for a fact that it's entirely possible to learn to celebrate the life you have—single or not. And once the attitude of celebration enters the picture, you'll be on your way to the life of your dreams. Life alone is cause for celebration. If you're single, go ahead and join the party!

65

FIND YOUR OWN WAY

Women who grow up in this century have many options, and with options come choices. However, we now have so many options that the difficulty, and often the struggle, occurs in the choosing. It's truly ironic that for the last one hundred years, our grandmothers and great-grandmothers fought and struggled so that women in future generations would have choices; yet here we sit, often confused about our roles and about balancing career and family. There are no clear-cut paradigms for women today, and therefore we must pioneer once again and find our own way.

I remember my anxiety upon graduating from college. I wasn't sure what I really wanted to do for a career, yet I felt as if I should know what I was going to do with my life. I know that if Richard and I hadn't married right out of college, I'd have been in New York, trying to find a job in advertising. In some ways, getting married "young" confused me even more, and muddled my preconceived notions about being career-driven.

I felt very alone while searching for a job in advertising in San Francisco. Eventually, I put the search on hold. I knew I would make such a great receptionist that it might take me forever to work my way up the ladder. It wasn't until I decided to get my massage certification and explore the field of healing arts that my path became clear—although not exactly what you would expect. Nearing the end of the certification, with my scant graphic design background, I put together some business cards. As I began to pass them out to the other class members, they were so impressed they asked me if I would design some for them. Voilà! Suddenly I found myself in the business of graphic design. It wasn't long before I was doing newsletters and annual reports for medium-sized businesses and banks. I opened up shop, hired a couple of designers, became "Graphically Yours," and eventually "Kris Carlson and Associates: A Marketing Design Group." And, you know what? I was a damn good receptionist, as well as account executive and production manager! I wore lots of hats, cried a little at the intense deadines and client conflicts, and had loads of fun while clearing my overhead and making some profit.

There can be tremendous stress in options; we finally figure out what career we want to pursue, then eventually we get married, and a few years later we have a child. What do we do now? Our choices are no longer so clear-cut.

Currently, we have no clear-cut model for women who blend career and raising a family. This means that, once again, women find themselves in a pioneer role on a new frontier. When mapping out your role as a woman, your best strategy is to find your own way. You have to consider your own finances and value system, and what works best for you and your family. Once you make choices, though, don't think of yourself as a victim. "You've come a long way, baby," and you do have options.

Find your own way, and continue to evaluate your choices. When things are humming right along and everyone is satisfied, enjoy the ride while you're coasting. As things change, consider your options once again, and remember how fortunate you are to have them. While it can be trying to make choices, not having them is far worse!

66

ALLOW ENTHUSIASM TO BUBBLE UP FROM YOU

Allowing enthusiasm to bubble up from you and pervade your very existence will bring an abundance of joy to yourself and others. It's one of the simplest ways I can think of to serve others. Sharing a natural good feeling which comes from inside feels great, and is contagious.

Enthusiasm is a key ingredient of success—in everything from business, to a project with the PTA, or helping your toddler learn to walk. Even if you're feeling low, notice how much better you feel if you can muster a smile, better yet a laugh, or greet someone enthusiastically.

I have a dear friend who allows enthusiasm to bubble up from her. She greets the grocery clerk at her supermarket with as much kindness and warmth as she would give a close friend. She looks directly into her eyes and smiles warmly from her heart. With genuine caring, she asks, "How are you, anyway?" This kind of enthusiasm improves the day of every person she greets.

Some people are quiet in their approach to enthusiasm; others are more demonstrative. While some people might find too much enthusiasm overwhelming, even they will admit that it's inspiring to hang around people who are genuinely interested in what they have to say and who are enthused about life.

Recently a friend of mine told me that she was going to start a business. I wasn't particularly interested in the product that she planned to distribute, but I reflected her enthusiasm for her new venture. I could have told her it would never work, that there was a lot more to this than met the eye, and so on. But rather than bring up the possible negatives, I made suggestions that would encourage and support her on her path. I mirrored her enthusiasm back to her.

There are always two ways to look at the same thing: You can see the glass as half empty or as half full. It is important to recognize your own habit of thinking. A habit of enthusiasm is a healthy and nourishing way to think. If you see that you have a choice in how you view a situation, generally you can always find something positive.

As you express your enthusiasm, people will share their dreams and inspirations with you because they know it will put them in a place of strength to do so. It feels good when others trust you to support their vision. It's a small way to share heartfelt joy, and it's also a way to reduce your own stress. Not only do you feel better, but the people around you will be more upbeat and positive, as well.

67

SHARE THE "NICE" STORIES

It seems that as a culture, we are preoccupied with the negative stories in our own lives and in the world around us. The media "works" a newsbreaking story till it's dead, and we immerse ourselves in the pathos of others.

Have you ever been at a baby shower when someone shared how wonderful the birth process is? Generally, we hear the many horror stories that women have about their ordeal; just what a first-time mother needs as inspiration prior to childbirth!

Our children come home from school and fail to mention what a good day they had, but instead we hear about the negative incident that happened on the playground with a friend, or how mean their teacher was today. Wouldn't it be a great thing if we shared more of the "nice" stories?

Last weekend, Richard and I watched the movie, *The Story of Us*. While it was anything but uplifting, the family in the story did one really great thing at dinnertime. They shared their personal "high" for the day and their personal "low." This is a great idea because it encourages some very healthy reflective thinking. It also provides for some uplifting conversation during dinner, as well as the usual venting.

One of the kindest things you can do for another person is to share a nice story with a parent about their child. There is nothing that makes me feel better than to hear of a good deed that one of my children did. Often we only hear from people when our children are in some sort of conflict.

One day at school, a mother pulled me aside and said, "Did you hear what Jazzy did today at school?" Well, I don't know about you, but even though Jazzy rarely gets into major mischief, when I hear that I think, "Oh, no! What did Jazzy do?" This woman laughed at my expression and with tears in her eyes told me that Jazzy had intervened and caught the arm of another child who had her daughter pinned against the wall. The other child had been ready to throw a punch at her daughter's face. I have never been so proud of Jazzy, and it warmed my heart to hear of her courage.

A friend of mine, Sandra, has a daughter who sometimes gets pegged as a troublemaker. Katie happens to have a functional form of autism, and her behavior is often misinterpreted by grownups and children who don't understand her disability or don't know she has one. Sandra tires of explaining Katie's plight to people she barely knows. One day she shared with me how another mother called her up, out of the blue, and told her how helpful Katie was that day in the classroom. This conversation brightened Sandra's spirits tremendously.

This strategy also applies at work. If we would practice building our peers up, and realize how much better we ourselves look in the process, most companies would have a much more satisfying atmosphere. One of the greatest things you can do for a coworker is to share with his or her boss something positive they did that was special or over and above what they are paid to do. Don't be afraid to build someone else up. Not only is it a kind thing to do, but it will make you look secure and as pure as sunshine, as well.

So, the next time you witness something great that a coworker accomplishes, or see someone's child (or your own) doing a good deed, be sure to pass on the positive news. Sharing the "nice" stories from your day is a proven stress-reliever, and will bond the members of your family more closely together, as well.

68

SAY "NO, BUT THANKS FOR ASKING" (WITHOUT FEELING GUILTY)

Here's an important strategy for all women who do too much! When you've hit your limit on how much you can do, and do with joy, it's imperative to your well-being to learn to say, "No, but thanks for asking." And it's important to learn to say these words without feeling any sense of guilt whatsoever.

Before you can apply this strategy, however, you'll probably want to evaluate, and come to terms with, exactly what your limits are: What you're able to do, what you're willing to do, and what you want to do.

The problem with taking on more committees, responsibilities, and leadership activities than you really have time for, is that eventually you will hit your limit—very suddenly—in the form of burnout and resentment.

All of a sudden, you'll have so much going on that you won't know how to turn back. You'll feel exhausted and overwhelmed, perhaps even resentful and bitter because too much has once again fallen into your lap. Your failure to say "No" without feeling guilty will have created a nightmare for yourself.

When you belong to an organization, of course you need to do your part. However, you can pick and choose based on what's going on in your life and the number of commitments you already have. You need to give yourself permission to say that enough is enough.

When you begin to acknowlege all that you do accomplish, your guilt will subside. There is tremendous power in knowing that you aren't buried with burdens your heart isn't really into. A clearer mind and a slightly more manageable schedule allows you to make decisions from a place of clarity rather than from a place of frantic desperation.

As you learn to say no without guilt, the events in which you do play a leadership role will give you greater joy and gratification. Not to mention that as you stop overextending yourself, you will do a finer job on those things in which you choose to participate.

Once you decide to decline the offer, it's best to do so without offering a litany of reasons why you can't. (That's a clue that you're feeling guilty.) Have you ever noticed that you lose the person's attention once you launch into the "why." People aren't interested in your busyness—they're contending with too much busyness of their own.

"People pleasers" find it most difficult to say no. They want to be liked so badly, they'll gladly sacrifice their own well-being. However, if you have to back out at the last minute because of other commitments, you aren't going to be liked very much. It's better not to commit in the first place than to leave someone in the lurch!

Learning to say "no" to your work, whether you own your own business or are an employee, is important, too. Remember that if you work long past 5:30 every night, you're cutting short your time with your husband and/or your children. Again, it's a question of balance. A good way to think of it is: Refuse to work those hours you aren't being paid for (i.e., late evenings and weekends).

You may also be tempted by your guilt to over-commit your social calendar. However, you'd better be on the same page as your spouse, boyfriend, or significant other, or your guilty "yesses" could cause you more frustration than you bargained for. Your partner may have a completely different social agenda and set of priorities. They may not appreciate doing things simply because you feel guilty!

Keep in mind that you may not be wasting only your own time by making commitments based on guilt, but also the people you say yes to. After all, would they really want to spend time with people who are only with them out of obligation and guilt?

So, the next time someone asks you if you'd like to chair a committee, organize a fundraiser, go on a field trip, work in a classroom, or even go out to dinner, take a moment to reflect. Honestly contemplate whether you really have the desire and the spare time before giving them an answer. If you feel as if you're overextended, or the timing is simply off, simply say, "No, but thanks for asking," and leave it at that.

69

GIVE YOURSELF MORE TIME THAN YOU THINK YOU'LL NEED

In a way, this is an obvious point, but it's certainly worth repeating. There's no question that one of the greatest causes of day-to-day stress is the constant rushing around due to the simple fact that we don't allow ourselves enough time. The truth is, it usually takes a little longer to get from one place to the next than we think it's going to.

Our intentions are certainly not harmful. When we wait too long to leave, or when we don't allow enough time in between activities, we usually do so only because we're trying to get just a little more work done or do one more thing before we leave. We squeeze in one more phone call, or dump one more load of laundry into the washer. So we either don't leave when we should, or we don't get ready—at least all the way ready—quite early enough.

It's as if we deny the reality of how long it takes to actually get somewhere, door to door. We neglect to factor in traffic, parking, unexpected delays, the time it takes to walk from the car or subway, and so forth. We assume that everything is going to go perfectly, which of course, it rarely does. So whether we're going from one meeting to another, picking up the kids from school, or driving to the airport, we simply wait just a little too long, and, predictably, every single time, we end up adding to our stress.

Getting ready early and leaving plenty of time takes an enormous amount of stress out of our lives. Instead of rushing, we relax. Instead of worrying, we are calm and secure. Rather than keeping others waiting, we're on time. We spend less time apologizing and making excuses. Instead of always wondering "what's next?", we're able to be slightly more present. Having plenty of time can mean the difference between enjoying something and dreading it. When you're rushing, it's impossible to enjoy what you're doing because almost by definition, you're wishing you were somewhere else.

The importance of getting ready early and allowing a bit more time in-between things goes even deeper. In a subtle way, it encourages you to schedule fewer activities so you end up less overwhelmed. It's a preventive measure. Because you are allowing slightly more space in-between, and plenty of time to get to and from, your calendar is less crowded. Instead of thinking you can squeeze ten things into a day, you assume differently. You remind yourself that, in reality, you can only do eight, or whatever. So in a way, you're giving yourself a "time rebate." Instead of spending all of your time "doing" and "going," you put a little of that available time in-between. You can think of it as time for you.

70

GO WITH THE GIRLS

There are few experiences more empowering than getting a small group of select women together to enjoy a retreat weekend. A weekend with the girls, now and then, is filled with great food, wonderful wine, laughter, tears, and a lot of talking and walking.

Recently I went on a retreat with four friends. Sally, who is my good friend, was the only person who didn't know the others; she was visiting me from Seattle. We had chosen a house on the Pacific coast as our brief respite from kids, soccer, and all the thousands of things that busied our lives each day. When Sally arrived, everyone greeted her with a giddiness that spoke of high moods and the joy of knowing we had time to relax and play. We began to talk about the gourmet items we'd picked up that day, what was for dinner that evening, and the favorite wine we'd enjoy at sunset.

As the weekend unfolded, the depth of our conversation became astoundingly nourishing. Women have a way of finding the common ground we all stand on, and of delving into any topic to scrutinize it and evaluate it from all angles. We may not have agreed on every issue, but each woman at our retreat brought to the table her ideas and then silently listened as she passed the torch to the next player. When one cried, we cried together; when we laughed, we nearly peed in our pants! In this short time, we shared our joys, our heartaches, our hopes and dreams. We read inspirational books, we did watercolors, and we watched great movies and then talked till 2 A.M.

Without having to say it, there was an unspoken code of silence between us: All that was said here on this weekend was held sacred. There are no better nurturers than women, and for this short retreat, we each poured all our energies into nurturing each other. As we packed to go home, we felt a little bit sad at the ending of a great time, but we each felt renewed and refreshed, able to face our lives and families with new perspective.

If you can work out a retreat weekend, do it! It's worth the effort. If it's impossible, plan a girl's night out once in a while, which is an option open to most. The benefits will still be great. Make it a long evening, somewhere you can talk all night! Whatever form it takes, make it a point to go out with the girls every once in a while. It will help you recharge and be the best that you can be!

71

DON'T BECOME OVER-IDENTIFIED
IN ANY ROLE

It's tempting to classify ourselves as a product of all of our accomplishments and achievements. As women, we have a great challenge to not become over-identified in our roles, whether as mother, grandmother, career woman, or wife. It's easy in our culture to mistake doing for being. Wayne Dyer said it perfectly when he stated, "When you are what you do, then when you don't, you aren't." That's a powerful statement to ponder.

We are trained from an early age to identify ourselves as a certain "type" by our physical characteristics. You are either model-thin, "average," or plump and voluptuous. I, for example, being blonde, was determined not to be labeled a "dumb blonde." I worked my buns off in high school to get straight A's, driven to avoid this image.

We are also trained at a young age to have a resumé mentality—we are trained to become somebody or something. If you get on the honor roll, you're labeled a good student; otherwise, you're not. Just the other day I was working in Jazzy's fifth grade classroom and noticed a doodle on a girl's folder. There was her name, and directly under it, it said, "Cheerleader." I thought, wow, this happens very young: This girl already associates her identity with what she does.

I recently bumped into an acquaintance I had not seen in many months. When I asked her how she was, she launched into her busy schedule with her kids. Then I heard about all of their wonderful accomplishments and so on and so forth. I took a good look at her while she was talking, and it struck me how thin she had become. I also noticed that she looked exhausted. Her children had obviously become everything to her, and while her devotion to her family was an outstanding merit, she appeared to have little, if any, interests that revolved around herself. If she continues to live her life in this manner, it won't do her sons and daughters any good if she keels over from fatigue or burnout.

It seems that mothers have the greatest challenge in applying this strategy because raising children can be so all-consuming. It's easy to think of yourself as "a mom," sometimes forgetting that you're also a "human being." It's no wonder so many women suffer from the empty nest syndrome later in life when their children leave home. By over-identifying with any role—no matter how wonderful the role is—you box yourself into a corner and curtail your perception of who you are.

There is no limit to how much you can give of your time and energy to your family. You can constantly find ways to fill your life up with their activities and interests, but it still may seem like you're not doing enough. If you don't make limits, fit in some of your own interests, and discover more about yourself, you may wake up one day and wonder where "you" went. No one else can find that limit for you. We must find a balance between pursuing a few of our own interests, and fostering the interests of our families. Your children will eventually grow up and go on with their lives, and you need to create some space in your life for you.

Women who balance career and motherhood probably are the best at applying this strategy. They must be able to take one hat off and put another on, sometimes in nothing more than a moment's notice. Whether you are the main breadwinner in your family or not, chances are, when your child has a fever or breaks his arm, it's Mom he calls for. Your professional work may end at five, but your work as mother is never done. And it doesn't seem to matter to your children what your rank is at the office or whether you are a famous author or actress—to them, you're simply "Mom."

Until you come to terms with this notion that you aren't what you do, but rather a person who does many things, you may find yourself leading a complicated life. If you're over-identified with your career, you may decide that you simply could never raise a family, or you won't consider staying home with your children, even part-time. If you have several children and your youngest is pushing five or six, having another baby for fear of what you'll do with your time when your last goes to school may put both you and your family over the edge emotionally.

We all need to experience life as individuals, as well as to give to others, including our families. Your life experience will become all the more rich and rewarding as you learn to do many things without labeling yourself.

72

DEFUSE THE THOUGHT EXPLOSION!

You've had a tough day. In fact, you've had a tough week. Hang on, you've had a tough life! You're tired, worn down, irritated. You're feeling bothered and your head is filled with your list of things to do. In your low, exhausted mood, you're reminded of all the people who are depending on you. Maybe you're even feeling a bit taken advantage of. Richard's grandmother, Emily, always said, "It's a good life if you don't weaken," and she had a good point! There is much to wear us down if we let it.

In times like these, it's particularly important to recognize the incredible power of thought. The mere recognition of its power, and the simple acknowledgment of the role it plays during these times, can be a real lifesaver.

It seems that the time our minds really become involved in our lives is when we're the most overwhelmed. Such times leave us vulnerable. Bad enough that we're confused, going a mile a minute, not knowing which way is up. But this is precisely when our minds start spinning, usually in very negative directions. We analyze our lives, validate our frustration, and conjure up all sorts of worst-case scenarios in our heads. We make an iron-clad case in our minds to justify all the reasons why our lives are out of control. This is all a very fancy way of saying that we blow things—or should I say, "think things"—out of proportion. It's as though we're having an actual "thought explosion" right in our own minds!

The act of recognizing your own thinking is like waking up and seeing what's going on in your own head. It's almost like watching a movie—the difference being that it's your life, with all its frustrations, instead.

You can reduce the stressful effects of those thoughts by simply saying to yourself something like, "Wow, there I go again," or some other simple acknowledgment that you're the one doing the thinking that is creating (or at least compounding) the confusion. This awareness of your thinking breaks the chain, slows the process, and gives you a bit of needed perspective, a chance to regain your bearings. It's very empowering, because acknowledging yourself as the thinker also suggests that you're the one person who has the capacity to change, or at least take a bit less seriously, the content.

Again, this is not about pretending that your life is better than it is, or that you're any more "together" than you actually feel. Rather, it's acknowledging that things are difficult right now. At the same time, it's admitting that the only part of the picture you have any degree of control over (your own thoughts) is also playing a role in your frustration. As you begin to see how your thinking is exacerbating, building up, and dramatizing the problems and frustrations in your life, you'll feel a bit of relief. It's analogous to speeding down the highway with your "pedal to the metal" and suddenly taking your foot off the accelerator. You'll still be going too fast, at least for a few more moments, but you've taken the first step in slowing down.

Our thoughts are powerful tools. Luckily, many times we use them to our great advantage. Yet there are times, for all of us, when less really is better. I encourage you to "back off" and recognize your own thinking the next time you're feeling upset or overwhelmed. You might be pleasantly surprised at how quickly you'll feel better.

73

WHEN ALL ELSE FAILS, LAUGH

We've all had at least one of "those" days, if not many. I admit that my problems are minimal compared to most people, so indulge me as I share with you a day where Murphy's Law definitely applied to all sorts of "small stuff." Everything that could go wrong, did. The only solution to a day like that is to laugh.

I wake up in the morning one-half hour late to meet my running partner by 6:30 A.M. My oldest daughter, Jazzy, insists that I follow through with my promise of a four-color hair wrap prior to my run. I begin her hair wrap and ten minutes later, in her opinion, "It's all wrong." I take the whole thing out (which takes nearly as much time as it took to do it in the first place), all to convince her that I am willing to do it over again.

My running buddy shows up at the door and I'm still in my robe. I send her out with Ty, our dog, in hopes of catching her for a couple of miles on the way home. I'd really been counting on my run today, and I'm frustrated that I'm missing it. She returns just as I'm finishing up Jazzy's final wrap, still in my robe. She leaves. By then I'm too tired to run anyway.

Next I go over to the washing machine to get my clothes out and put them in the dryer. Not only are the laundry baskets missing (because someone likes to use them to carry his work stuff), but the same person (yeah, it was him) who was kind enough to help with the laundry, broke the cardinal rule of mixing the darks with the whites. All of my white lingerie and my favorite pink sweatshirt look a very muddy gray. I sit down on the floor and scream!

Then I realize that this is a perfect example of a day to write about—plenty of small stuff to let go of—and I know I have to laugh, because, after all, I am writing a book about not sweating the small stuff!

There you go. We've all had them. During those days where everything is going wrong, keep your sense of humor, and understand that no one is exempt from having days like "these" when it seems like everything that could go wrong—does.

Keep your perspective; after all, in most cases, it really could be worse. But chances are, if you use laughter as a release, you will see the humor in the really small stuff that goes wrong, and you will be well on your way to putting it behind you and having a happier day.

74

PLAN AN INSPIRATION FLOW DAY

We all live with such hectic and busy schedules that we forget that we are the master planner of these schedules. We become slaves to our Day-Timers. Okay, master planner, I dare you to look in your calendar right now and place one big large "X" on any one day. Commit to leaving it that way, in order to plan your "inspiration flow" day. On this day, you won't pre-plan any activities for you or anyone else in your family. You're going to have a day of pure inspiration where you simply take it one step at a time and do what occurs to you, moment to moment.

On your inspiration flow day, wake up in a leisurely manner. Don't jump out of bed as if you have a schedule to keep. Today, you don't. You're going to practice living by inspiration. When you open your eyes, what are your first thoughts? If your mind is already busy, take a few deep breaths to clear your head. Notice what bubbles up when you ask yourself, "How do I feel like spending my time today?" *Feel* is the key word here. Now is not the time to pull out your notepad and make a list, because you are going to live this day from moment to moment.

Take this day in baby steps and only do what occurs to you right now. If you want to take a walk, do it now. Don't plan it for later. Today, don't plan any part of your day in the morning. What occurs to you will constantly change, all day long. Just see what pops up, and then go ahead and do it!

Give yourself permission to indulge yourself for one day. If you feel like an ice cream sundae or chocolate cake for breakfast, go ahead. Or, perhaps you feel inspired to paint a room in your house. Maybe you want to stay in bed and have a pajama day. Or, maybe you want to go out to breakfast with your family.

On this day, stay away from the telephone. Practice living from moment to moment without feeling the pull of obligations. Be a child again and play, or be an adult and do a project. Spend some quality time with your kids doing "rainy day" art while the sun is shining. In short, live this day for this day only.

You might be wondering why you should do this. Inspiration is like anything else: to achieve it, you must practice tapping into it. There are many things you will learn. First of all, taking a day off gives you a feeling of total and utter freedom. For the first time in a long time, you can really feel like the master of your destiny, even if only for a day!

It might take you a little while to get used to this strategy and stick to it, depending on how structured a person you are, but my guess is, you'll like it. You'll still go to work on Monday or get the kids to school on time, and life will go on as usual for the next six days. The difference is that you will be more inspired in your work and have more patience with your kids. You'll also gain a really good perspective that lacks the frustration of centering your life around everyone but you.

I hope you enjoy this strategy as much as I do, and that you are able to find small ways to incorporate it into your daily life. Tapping into inspiration flow is the ultimate in experiencing the moment, and it sure makes life interesting and adventuresome—even if it's only for a day.

75

GRIPE TO THE ONE YOU'VE GOT
THE GRIPE WITH

Across the board, it seems that this is an area in which women struggle. The way it plays out is this: We have a gripe with a family member, neighbor, friend, or whomever. We get all caught up in whatever "small thing" is bugging us, and we go around the mulberry bush several times about the same issue. We end up talking about it with everyone except the one person who can really make a difference: the one we have the gripe with.

Sandy, a friend of mine, called me up the other day. After the hello's and how are you's, she launched into an issue which I could tell was a real burr in her side. She explained to me in great detail a common thing that happened weekly regarding carpooling with a neighbor woman and how frustrating it was that she couldn't count on her to do her part. I asked her why she didn't just bow out of the carpool, explaining her feelings, and coming up with a polite excuse. She said to me, "Ah well, it's really not that big a deal, and after all, she's my neighbor and I'm new to the community." What struck me was that the situation clearly had been bothering her for quite some time, and to her, it *was* a big deal. Yet what I learned from her response was that she was willing to suffer the consequences and frustration of an unreliable carpool participant, rather than risk making any waves, or risk not being liked by her neighbor.

Herein lies a real issue for those of us who are "the good girls." We become afraid of any sort of confrontation for fear of not being liked or rocking the boat. We would rather endure daily frustration, fester with seething resentment, than have the face-off we fantasize about with the one with whom we're upset.

The problem in dealing with frustration in this indirect manner is two-fold. First, the issue rarely gets resolved because the person with whom you have the issue is clueless that he or she is doing anything wrong. Whatever is going on may indeed be their fault, but you can't blame them forever if they aren't even aware that you're upset. You haven't given them the opportunity to mend their ways.

In addition, venting to others instead of to the person you actually have the gripe with makes the issue drag on and on like a slow death. By discussing it with others, you're constantly re-opening the wound and reminding yourself of your own frustration, if not downright validating it and building it up even bigger. You're not, however, doing anything constructive to resolve it. In a way, you're sweating the small stuff because you've not turned your concern into a legitimate issue with the right person.

How do we muster up enough courage to go ahead and say what's on our mind in a constructive non-defensive manner, to the person we actually have the gripe with?

The way I see it is this. If you really want to be liked by someone, as perhaps Sandy wants to be liked by her neighbor, respect is an integral part of that equation. Sandy will not receive much respect from her neighbor if she continues to bite her tongue and be a doormat. That respect will be further lessened should the neighbor hear rumors that Sandy is talking behind her back!

A better solution is this. The next time her neighbor has an excuse for why she can't follow through with her committment, Sandy can simply state, in a non-reactive tone, that, unfortunately, this carpool is no longer going to work for her. She can go on to explain (again, in a non-reactive tone) that from her perspective, a carpool must be a two-way street, as far as the commitment goes. She can explain that she absolutely understands that things come up from time to time, but that she must find someone who is more available on an ongoing basis to reciprocate. She doesn't have to be heated, angry, or upset; in fact, that would work against her. Instead, she merely needs to be factual and informative.

Sandy might find out that her neighbor has misunderstood what she expects out of the carpool, or she might find out she's been taken advantage of. Either way, she will have resolved the issue, and she won't feel stalemated in the same sour position.

Another thing to consider about a more serious set of gripes you may have (with your husband or family member, for example) is that through conflict, generally there comes a better understanding of whatever situation you're dealing with. This is especially true if those in conflict can discuss their feelings from a compassionate state of mind, perhaps having a heart-to-heart conversation. If not, you still might reach a clearer understanding.

No matter how hard you try to avoid it, conflict is a part of life. Even if you're not conflict-oriented by nature, you'll have little luck in escaping all of it.

So think of your gripes, especially the consistent ones (not to be confused with simple low-mood irritations), as an opportunity to have better communication with someone you care about or someone you're having to deal with. A' gripe or complaint is not a negative thing, but instead is a necessary and respectful form of clarification. When you gripe to the one you have the gripe with, you open the door to a two-way conversation which will help you both form a better understanding. You're demonstrating a great deal of respect for that person by offering them the chance to hear what you have to say and by giving them a chance to respond.

As you gain the confidence to say what's on your mind earlier, and especially to gripe to the one you have the gripe with, you'll be less resentful and all of your relationships will be clearer. Generally, there are two sides of a coin, and chances are, there's a simple misunderstanding that can be cleared up. The person you have the gripe with may have a legitimate excuse—or they may even have a gripe of their own. Either way is fine. And something to keep in mind is this. If someone doesn't like you, simply because you are being honest about your feelings, oh well, *C'est la vie!* Life goes on.

76

SPICE UP YOUR SEXY SIDE

Ladies, ladies, let's talk about lust. When was the last time you felt any? If you have to think about it, it's time to spice up your sexy side.

One of the consistent complaints that Richard and I hear from couples who are unhappily married is that generally most of life is great, except that their sex life has gone through several slumps, if not steadily gone downhill over the years. Often, after having children, it has become relatively non-existent. One of the partners—usually, but not always, the man—will say: "We had a great sex life before we were married or during our honeymoon phase of three years. Then it just came to a screeching halt!"

What happens to the sex drives of women, and sometimes men, after several years of marriage and after children? This is a question you must dare to ask yourself and also discuss as a couple, because it can become critical to the survival of your relationship. Often, it's a communication issue between partners. One partner may have a much higher sex drive than the other. In addition, there may be unresolved issues having nothing to do with sex that cause resentment to build over time. If this is the case, you may want to consider counseling. Once you get some of these issues off your chest and he understands you, you may feel a lot more attracted to him (and vice versa).

While sex is certainly not the end-all focus of a marriage—nor is it the ultimate expression about what it means to be truly intimate—it is invaluable to nurturing a lasting connection between two healthy individuals. I know it's a very personal topic, and there are many possible reasons for a lack of sex drive, including many that could be hormonal. (It's never a bad idea to get a medical opinion from your gynecologist.) But, barring a physical problem, it's worth the effort to have a healthy sexual relationship with your significant other.

On my wedding day, a man in his fifties who was an old family friend walked up to me and bestowed this advice: "You have a good man there, Kris. My advice to you is to keep him happy at home and he won't wander!" At first, I'll have to admit, I took offense at this. My thoughts were, "Yeah, well, he'd better keep me happy at home, too!" But I found out over time that the essence of what he was saying was right (for both men and women). People are sexual creatures; we need a lot of hugging, kissing, and touching. You can't entirely cut your husband off sexually and not expect him to crave attention elsewhere; the same, of course, would be true for you if he cut you off entirely.

I once heard a doctor on the radio proclaim that "Couples are just too tired to make sex a priority, anymore." Sometimes, raising our families and making ends meet financially simply take every last bit of our energy. And, if you are suffering from sleep deprivation (as in when you have young children), that certainly doesn't help in the intimate love department. There are times in all long-term relationships where sexual contact ebbs and flows; believe it or not, this is normal. You just don't want to let those "ebbs" drag on too long.

In our fifteen married years, Richard and I have been through a few ebbs and flows of our own. I remember a phase in our marriage when our own children were small, in which we began to joke about our lack of sex. I knew that he didn't want to pressure me or have to feel rejected if I was too tired. For awhile, he simply stopped pursuing it.

One day I woke up with a start and wondered what had happened to the spunky woman I used to be. The advice I'd received at our wedding came back to me. I knew I needed to spice up my sexy side, and to remember what I was like in the early years of our relationship.

What spices *you* up may be entirely different, but I happen to thrive on spontaneity. I decided that this would help me spice up my sexual side. I love to initiate a "surprise attack" in moments when he least expects it—and oh, how he loves to be surprised. Most men appreciate it if you take the initiative at least half the time. Once you have children running around, spontaneity becomes nearly impossible, so you must become very creative. And privacy locks on your doors are a must! If you have to plan, mention your idea in the morning and use the wait to tease him a little throughout the day. You'll be surprised how much the anticipation builds in both of you!

Here are a few if not original, hopefully inspirational ideas to spice up your sexy side: Show up in his office and lock the door—need I say more? Light candles all over your bedroom and wait for him in bed. Buy new panties and bras. The next time you plan a "date night," rent a hotel room for the evening instead of going to dinner and a movie. Don't worry, he won't mind your spending the extra money! Pinpoint where your passion is and reawaken that part of you that he has always been so attracted to. Let go of the serious, overly tired, dutiful, heavy-laden-with-responsibility side of yourself and lighten up. A heavy attitude is never sexy. Go ahead and have some fun!

If your sex life is adequate but you're looking for a stronger spiritual connection and a deeper union of intimacy, consider taking a tantric yoga workshop or reading a book together. Then . . . practice makes perfect.

The reality is, most couples who are happy, are having sex! There's no question that it is necessary to the survival of your long-term connection. So, it's up to you to take charge and spice up your sexy side. It'll keep you young, and you'll *both* be happy at home!

77

BE 99 PERCENT
GOSSIP-FREE

I considered calling this chapter "No More Gossip for Sport," but I don't like to advocate "doing as I say and not as I do." I realized that I'd be digging myself a hole I couldn't get out of, as it seems that nearly everyone—and I am no exception—partakes of gossip in one form or another. Try as I might to limit what I say about other people to other people, I realize that I'm more likely to have success in this area (and you might too) if the standard is to be 99 percent gossip-free.

The study of human behavior is far too interesting, it seems, to keep our observations and hearsay to ourselves! When we're really honest with ourselves, don't you think we find a sense of safety and relief in sharing something juicy that's happening to someone else? We're grateful, as our mouths are saying the words, that it's them and not us. It also seems that we're more prone to gossip about people we aren't that fond of, or perhaps are a bit envious of, for one reason or another (and this probably isn't something we'd be willing to admit).

Our need for gossip could stem from a bit of boredom with what's happening—or not happening—in our own lives. We may attempt to appear more interesting to someone we're talking to by having the "hottest" news.

I had a college roommate who left a dramatic impression on me. We used to spend long hours talking about everything from boys to the spiritual side of life. Occasionally, as someone's name would come up, I would begin to make an observation about this person. She would stop me dead in my tracks, put her hands over her ears, and proclaim: "I won't speak or hear anything about another person that is mean or potentially not true!" This would crack me up, and truthfully, there were times when, just to check her consistency, I would test her on purpose. But to no avail—she was committed 100 percent to this rule! I had nothing but the greatest admiration for her. She set such a great example, and I knew I could trust her with any secret.

Unless you want to be known for being a gossip who will say anything to anyone, try to limit your gossip to one friend, as I do, and even then, don't indulge in it too often. Be 99 percent gossip-free, and whatever you say, don't ever gossip about the one friend you gossip to!

78

HAVE A BACKUP DAY CARE PLAN

If it's not stressful enough handling both a career and motherhood, finding and keeping quality child care providers is enough to make you change your mind about your work altogether. Women who must leave their children in the care of someone else endure one of the greatest stresses of all time: Finding someone that they trust with the most important part of their life—their children. Once you finally find someone you trust, you feel an instant sense of relief. But even the best babysitters have days where they need to miss work, either from sickness, appointments or such.

A typical scenario is this: you're planning to drop your child at the sitter's and then rush to work, having a 9:15 meeting, then an 11:00 appointment, then a business luncheon. At 8:00 that morning, your sitter calls to say that she has the flu. Or your child is in group day care, and he becomes ill during the night. You can't send him out sick, so someone has to stay home with him. And who is it who stays home with your child, having to reschedule all her office appointments? Most times (but not always), it's the woman of the household; she is, after all, "Mom."

Some smart women I know have found that they need a backup person for their babysitter. You might consider this strategy, as well. That way, if for some reason the sitter can't watch your child, you have a reliable person to call. It's great if that backup person is a relative, but with families scattered all over the country the way they are now, that may be unrealistic. Finding someone who can be available at the last minute can be difficult, but given that the situation isn't going to occur more than a few times a year (one would hope), it shouldn't be impossible. It's important to keep in touch with that person from time to time, even if you're not using her childcare services very often. Call her just to say hello and to remind her that you're still counting on her if and when an emergency happens. This way, when the moment arrives, you won't be calling her out of the blue.

Another alternative is to take turns with your spouse: one time he stays home from work; the next time, you do it. Then at least every single time your sitter isn't available, you aren't the one who has to turn your day upside down. Or you may arrange it so you'll do most days, but your husband fills in when you have a very important client meeting, for in-stance.

The more expensive idea—but one that works if you're really des-perate—is to keep the number of a nanny service that you have checked out beforehand near the phone. You may have to pay a higher hourly rate, but if you just can't get out of work that day, it's a possible solution. Perhaps you have a good friend who doesn't work out of the house, and who will fill in for you in a pinch. (In these instances, you should plan to reciprocate for her on evenings or weekends, every time she helps you out.) It's a good idea to do this sooner rather than later. You may even take this backup concept one step further and have a backup for your backup!

Either way, it's important that you're not left hanging when your child or your babysitter becomes ill. If you have to be at work, you don't want to be sweating it about who's taking care of your child. Because after all, that's your most important priority.

79

DON'T WEIGH EVERY DAY

The most balanced women, as far as their body image goes, rarely weigh themselves. They refuse to get too focused on their weight. On the other hand, some women only have a "good" day when the scale tips below a certain number. I fall somewhere in the middle. One of my personal struggles has revolved around my tendency to become obsessed with diet and exercise.

I used to weigh myself every day. Always after my run and fully naked, I would step on the scale, hold my breath, and see what the outcome would be. Weighing became a barometer of how I would feel that day. Talk about small stuff; a pound less, and I would feel elated! A pound more, and I would feel depressed.

Fortunately, one day, my scale broke. It was several weeks before I replaced it. As I was forced to give up my habit, I realized that I felt much better when I didn't weigh every day. I could see that this simple habit was feeding my tendency to be overly concerned with my body and how I looked. I felt much happier and more peaceful eliminating a very small habit that had grown very large in my mind.

A good friend of mine struggled with the same habit. She would be very excited if she lost a pound or two, and conversely would be very low if she had gained. I explained to my friend that I used to weigh every day, too. I asked her if she was automatically bummed out if the sun wasn't shining when she woke up. She laughed at me and said, "Of course not." We talked about how it felt better to feel lighter, but the reality was this; allowing ourselves to be trapped by the false high we would feel on the days we weighed less was like allowing the weather to dictate how we would feel that day.

It's all right to care about how you look, and it is certainly a good idea to take care of your health by eating right and squeezing in time for exercise. It is, however, self-defeating and obsessive to step on a scale every day. You will find greater peace and contentment when you let such obsessive behavior go.

80

MERGE THE SPIRITUAL AND
MATERIAL WORLDS

With all the trappings of living in the material world, this strategy is often easier said than done. From an early age, many of us are taught that acquiring things, searching out exciting experiences, and collecting achievements will make us happy. And while there is certainly nothing wrong with any of these things—they can be an enriching part of life—it's important to know that, ultimately, none of them in and of themselves will make you happy.

If you take a step back, it's fairly obvious that if things were going to make you feel complete, they already would have! After all, most of us have already achieved many of our previous goals that were "going to make us happy." We've acquired a treasured possession(s) that was "going to bring us joy and a feeling of security," and we've had many exciting experiences that were "going to bring us satisfaction." And while we may have experienced these results to some small degree, we are, nevertheless, still longing for more. Somehow, we just keep hoping that the next thing on the list will do the trick.

Often, when we travel to other parts of the world, we become acutely aware of how rich we Americans are materially, yet how lacking we are spiritually.

Richard and I had the eye-opening experience of traveling to India a number of years ago. While I thought I had mentally prepared myself, I was, in reality, astounded at the level of poverty in which many people in the big cities lived. It hit us in our hearts, and gave us a perspective like none other, on just how much we have materially, yet how we often still feel the need to strive for more. In other words, the things (stuff, achievements, money, experiences) didn't automatically lead to a feeling of satisfaction—that part had to come from within.

On the surface, it would seem that we have the greatest opportunity to pursue our spiritual nature when our physical needs for survival are met. As Maslow's Hierarchy of Needs reminds us, as our basic needs are met, our attention and efforts are freed up so that we may devote our energies to the deeper needs of being human, as well as to our spiritual life. However, the opposite often turns out to be the case. Most of us seem to get so caught up in our material wants and desires, as well as our ambitions and our need for more, more, more, that we ignore our spiritual selves in favor of physical comforts and instant gratification.

On the other hand, a country such as India may be among the richest spiritual cultures in the world, despite the enormous physical hardships endured by a vast majority of its people. Why is this?

It's possible that in a culture that historically has had a caste mentality, many people lack the hope of pursuing material dreams or financial security. This could be due, in part, to their belief that people are born into their circumstances; that their lives are pre-destined. Perhaps this situation frees them up to explore the inner spiritual realm. While in India, many shared with me the obvious yet powerful truth that the ability to nurture one's spirit, to embrace one's spirituality, and to turn inward, is free to all—independent of one's circumstances.

On the other hand, those of us with extreme good fortune, from a material perspective, have not often experienced this bliss from the inside out. Instead, many of us live with the notion that financial freedom and the acquisition of our physical desires is where bliss will be found. But again, if financial freedom were bliss, then why are so many people who acquire it absolutely miserable?

I'm not making the case for voluntary poverty. Yet, from my perspective, one of our true spiritual challenges is to awaken to the fact that we are given the distractions of a material world, in part, in order to see beyond it; to be able to live with conveniences without being overly dependent on them; to be able to acquire things without being greedy or unethical; to be able to enjoy and appreciate nice things without neglecting the beauty of simplicity and of nature; and to realize that, in the end, none of the "things" really matter anyway.

Along the same lines, we can use the challenges of a material world to help us grow and become better people. For example, owning a computer is a material convenience, but when it crashes, do you freak out, or can you use that experience to heighten your perspective? When you go out to your favorite restaurant and it's closed on Monday night, can you remember how truly blessed you are to have the expendable income to go out at all? We can use most, or even all of our day-to-day experiences, including the hassles, as validation that life isn't meeting our expectations—or we can use them to grow, become more patient and more loving.

What really matters, of course, is how well we learn to love—ourselves, each other, nature, our communities, the world, and our God or spiritual entity. On our deathbeds, few of us will be saying, "Gee, I wish

I had been more uptight," or, "I wish I had collected just a few more things." Instead, most of us will acknowledge that sweating the small stuff—being bothered so much of the time—wasn't really worth it. Life is short, and is too wonderful to waste it being concerned with trivial frustrations.

While it's okay to enjoy your material blessings, and it's certainly desirable to work hard so that you and your loved ones can enjoy them and feel secure, the important thing to realize is that, if you want to be happy, they are not the end-all. When merging the physical, material world with your spiritual world, there are a number of questions you can ask yourself. How well do you live by the spiritual principles and values you ascribe to? Do you pass the daily challenges that emerge to test your values? Is Sunday the only day you devote a small amount of attention to your spiritual practice? How well do you merge your spiritual principles with your career?

In order to feel content, we must find a way to merge our spiritual selves into our material world. We are, after all, spiritual beings having a human experience! Because the details of our lives are so different, the way this strategy unfolds will vary from person to person. I'm confident, however, that with some heartfelt reflection, you'll be able to merge the two. And when you do, it will be worth it!

81

KNOW WHEN TO TURN OFF YOUR TECHNOLOGY BOOBY TRAPS

Remember how we used to call television the boob tube (didn't you just hate that expression?) because it began to take over our lives in such an obsessive fashion? Well, the high-tech revolution has taken over in very much the same way. It's important to see when your advanced communication devices actually limit your freedom, enslaving you instead of providing new opportunities for growth.

We have a choice: We can allow technology to work for us to help create more time and space for living, or we can become trapped in its speed, which perpetuates our need to get more done in one day. It is easy to forget the fact that Richard so poignantly points out in his original book, *Don't Sweat the Small Stuff:* "When you die, your in basket won't be empty." It's never going to all get done, so how much of your precious life energy will you sacrifice in your effort?

At the onset of the computer age, we were promised that we would become more efficient with the new technology, thereby gaining more leisure time. But in fact, we have become more frenetic, multi-tasked and speeded up—due, in part, to pagers, mobile phone systems, faxes, and, of course, the Internet and e-commerce revolution. It often seems that with cell phones, there's never an excuse not to return calls, even when you're on vacation or taking some time with your kids. These things were meant to give us more time and a higher quality of life, not take over our lives!

You can, however, make a different choice and set a new standard for your work habits by allowing technology to work for you; to create more time for living as opposed to more time devoted to doing more work. For example, women often complain that they have too little time to talk with their school-aged kids. Why, then, do so many parents use the time when they're taking their kids to and from school as an opportunity to talk on their cell phones, thus spending the time with someone else? That fifteen-minute drive can be your chance to connect with your kids and give them your full attention.

Technology can become detrimental to your quality of life when you use the time it saved to get more work done. You might find yourself with no limit on the number of calls you return in a day. Instead of limiting your cell phone use to returning calls on your way home from work so that, once you arrive home, you can be present with those you love, you leave it on even while attending your son's baseball game. Or the minute you walk in the door, you turn on your laptop to check your e-mail, instead of sharing heartfelt conversation with your children and spouse. We have allowed technology to run us at a faster and faster pace. But where on earth do we think we are racing to?

Like anything else in life, as we strive for balance, we can allow technology to work for us by setting appropriate limits and not falling into the booby traps. Consider the appropriate times to turn off your pager and cell phone altogether. This is especially true if you are a working mom and you want to free up time to spend with your spouse and children.

Don't allow yourself to become a slave to the devices that are meant to be a convenience for you. Beware of allowing the speeded-up pace of technology to seduce you away from balance. As you allow technology to work for you to truly become more efficient, you will get more done in the same amount of time; you don't need to get even more done! Technology should be a friend, not an enemy; when used properly, it will increase your quality of life, ease your hurried pace, and allow you more time to be present with those you care for most.

82

DON'T LET YOUR ANGER
GET THE BEST OF YOU

We are presented with hundreds of opportunities to apply this strategy. This is one that you may find extremely helpful, especially in communicating with someone with whom you are in conflict.

If you have had to hire a contractor to help you build or maintain your home or apartment, you'll understand the inherent frustrations in working with many of them. Last year we had the not-so-pleasurable, in fact nasty, experience of having our septic tank fail. After a long battle with both the environmental health agency as well as the city sewage agency, we opted to go for a sewage hookup. This required us to send a pipe from our house down a rather long hill, and install a pump station there to pump our household waste up yet another hill to a street about 400 feet away. This was a costly solution; however, we felt it was the more permanent one.

Little more than one year later, we started having problems with our pump station. It took several days to get the contractor out to look at it, and another week to get the "specialist" out to solve it. Supposedly, they took care of the problem.

I was recently walking past the pump station to help a neighbor plant some flowers when the smell informed me that it was malfunctioning once again. You can imagine that my initial reaction was not happy. Quite the contrary: I stormed up the hill, ready to threaten the contractor with a lawsuit. Instead, I took a few deep breaths and reminded myself not to let my anger get the best of me, since no one responds well to a personal attack. In fact, just the opposite is true. When treated with respect even in an ugly situation, most people will respond with integrity and do what they can to rectify a poor situation. This is exactly what happened as I calmly relayed the situation to the contractor. Within one-half hour, the specialist showed up to assess the new problem.

By not allowing your anger to get the best of you, you can channel your anger into solving the problem. Your determination will convey this to whomever you are communicating your message. If anger gets the best of you, you might as well be a runaway cannon because you will blow your solution out of reach. It is always a better idea to attack a situation with a level attitude; hotheads generally don't get much accomplished because people won't comply under such derogatory conditions. Many people would rather fight back than admit they are wrong when attacked. When you are firm but nonreactive, you will get the response you desire.

Of course, the same is true when dealing with your spouse or children. For instance, if you blow up at your kids for not cleaning up their rooms, they probably will just shrug you off (particularly if they're teenagers). But if you talk to them rationally about why you can't be expected to pick up after them, given everything else that you have to do, many kids will behave much more responsibly. They may not keep their room to your level of neatness, but they'll probably manage to straighten up to their own standards, at least more so than if you were constantly yelling at them about it.

Learning to be less reactive doesn't only relieve the stress of those you're reacting to; it makes your life much less stressful and more peaceful, as well. In fact, deciding not to allow your anger to get the best of you may be one of the most important decisions you ever make.

83

SEIZE YOUR OPPORTUNITIES

I've noticed an extraordinary correlation between those women who seize their opportunities to get out, take a break, or get away—and those who are happy, relaxed, and satisfied. I'm specifically referring to those women who not only look forward to taking some time for themselves, but who also follow through when the opportunity presents itself. Unfortunately, the reverse also seems to be true. Those women who avoid, postpone, neglect, or make excuses for the reasons they "can't" or "shouldn't" take time for themselves often feel burned out, stressed, depleted, even resentful.

It can be reassuring to know that you are a woman who isn't afraid to take an occasional rest, or even an all-out adventure. Whether it's a night on the town, a trip to the bookstore, a walk in the woods, or a weekend away, alone or with friends—time away from your responsibilities is an emotional and spiritual necessity.

Here's what's most interesting to me. While most women may agree that time away is important, there are nonetheless many who will somehow find a way to not do it. I've known many women who actually have plenty of opportunities, but won't recognize them. For example, a friend will invite such a person out for an evening. Or someone will suggest they go away together for a weekend, or on some sort of a trip. Or maybe she would love to schedule a day to be by herself, doing whatever. Yet, rather than say, "Great, let's do it" (or I'll do it), she will say, "I'd love to, but I've got too much to do," or "It's not a great time."

The problem is, as valid as her reasons may be, deep down, she knows she'd love to take a break. But rather than do what is necessary to make it happen, she skips the fun, violates her own need for a rest, and then—consciously or unconsciously—resents it. I know this is true, because I hear about it all the time. Women are always telling me, "God, I wish I'd go out more or do more for myself."

I knew a woman who was constantly longing for some time away from her kids. When friends or family would say, "Hey, I'd love to have your kids for the weekend," she would politely say, "Thanks, but this isn't a good time." It was never the right weekend; there was always a good reason. Then, the next time I'd see her, she would either complain about how exhausted she was, or she would talk about how wonderful it would be—and how lucky some women are—to somehow find a way to "escape" with their husbands. She had plenty of opportunities, but never seized them.

Obviously, you can't, nor would you want to take every opportunity that comes your way (unless they are truly rare). Yet, if you're in the habit of dismissing opportunity as it comes your way, you're going to miss out on the chance to have a more balanced life. So pay close attention to those opportunities to get away or take a break. You may be delighted at how good you're going to feel.

84

WIDEN YOUR SCOPE AND GET
SOME PERSPECTIVE

When you're feeling down and focusing on "small stuff," and life just isn't measuring up to all your hopes and dreams, it often helps to downsize your problems by widening your scope. You can enlarge your perspective to include a grander scheme of things. Your vision will become clearer as your problems are reduced to their proper "small stuff" place. The best way I know to adjust my expectations is to compare them to the bigger picture that life offers us.

Your vision of the world can be analogous to a camera taking photographs. You can zoom in and focus for a closeup shot, or use a wide-angle lens and see a bigger picture. When you focus on a specific problem, life seems very tenuous and difficult. However, as you compare your small stuff problems to the big stuff that happens around the world, you widen your scope and gain perspective; you are able to see just how small your own problems really are in comparison.

It's easy for all of us to get in the habit of focusing our attention on ourselves, forgetting about those who are less fortunate. For instance, women who become obsessed about their weight can pour all their energy into becoming thin. Their looks and bodies become everything to them, and they lose sight of the larger picture. These women, young and old, allow their lives to becomes a small black dot on a large white page. They think life is the small black dot, which represents their intention to become thin, whereas the opposite is true: Life is the greater white space on the page. The same principle applies if you focus too much on what you don't have, or on the one piece of furniture you are missing, or the blouse that you are yearning for. You will lack gratitude for all that you do have. If you find yourself focusing on the small stuff you don't have, it's a sign that perhaps you have temporarily clouded your vision and are lacking perspective. You might consider making a trip down to the local homeless shelter or food kitchen to help you regain your appreciation.

Watching the news ought to help everyone to size down their problems and gain some perspective. Some of the gripes and complaints we have in the U.S. are really small compared to what other nations must deal with. During the Kosovo war, for instance, I actually felt grateful to pay our taxes. Taxes are a small price to pay for the incredible luxury of living in a nation free from political oppression and all the tragedy that war brings with it.

When you are feeling low about your finances, it helps to remember that there are many people who don't have food to eat, much less a roof over their heads. The mere fact that you are able to read this book—or any book, for that matter—indicates that you have some degree of good fortune.

Did you know that there are more stars in the universe than all the grains of sand on every imaginable beach? The next time you find yourself worrying about a ding on your car, an unreturned phone call, the never-ending laundry pile, whether or not you are ever going to remodel your kitchen, or anything else that falls into the minutiae category, think how small these concerns are when comparing them to the larger picture of the stars in the universe. Widen your scope to see the greater image, and quit viewing life with tunnel vision. Your enlarged vision will be clearer and your experience here more peaceful and gratifying.

85

RENEGOTIATE YOUR BOUNDARIES

Just as it would be a bit selfish to be angry at someone because he or she has changed or grown in some way, it's also a disservice to yourself to not allow yourself the same privilege.

Women are constantly changing, both inside and out. We aren't the same people we were twenty years ago, ten, five, or even one. Our circumstances are as different as are our bodies. So are our preferences. Our needs are different, too—as are our interests. We've grown, changed, and, hopefully, evolved.

Given the nature of change, it would be crazy to have the identical boundaries that were appropriate at a different phase of your life. But the problem is, many people don't want us to change. Instead, they want us to be exactly the same as we always have been, especially those closest to us—our spouse, parents, boyfriend, children, and friends. They don't want us to create new boundaries, and they certainly aren't going to do it for us. In fact, they may put up a bit of a fuss. After all, there is a degree of comfort in predictability. And when people are comfortable, the last thing they typically embrace is change.

But despite any difficulties you may face in setting new boundaries, it's well worth any effort it takes. To create new boundaries means you are being honest with your needs and sharing with others what it takes for you to feel nourished. In the end, you'll be happier and more fulfilled, and so will those whom you love. This is the law of nature that says: When I'm happy, I'm a lot more fun to be around. I'm also more nurturing, loving, and helpful. When I have established the boundaries I need, I'm kinder, gentler, more generous, even sexier. Very simply, I'm an all-around better person.

It's important to acknowledge that a boundary isn't something that is negative. Everyone has boundaries; it's simply a question of where you draw them. For example, everyone needs time alone—it's just a matter of how much. Some need very little, others a great deal. Setting a boundary is like establishing a limit. It's like a line in the sand that says, "You can go this far, but no further."

I once met a grandmother of ten. She said that her first six grandchildren had her full and undivided attention. She established a way of being with her sons and daughters that said, "Bring the kids over any time you'd like. I'm always available." But, she said, by the time grandchild number seven came along, she was ready for a change. "Don't get me wrong," she told me, "I love all my grandchildren equally. It's just that for the first time in my life, I realized that I wanted to do a little traveling—not all the time, mind you—but a little bit. I needed some time for me."

The questions are: Is she obligated to remain exactly the same? Is it selfish of her to want to establish some new boundaries? Not if you ask me. Far from being selfish, she was still spending a great deal of time with her grandkids. She made it abundantly clear that she loved every one of them. She still did things with them, attended special events, welcomed them into her home, and was obviously very proud of each of them. Yet, the truth was, she had changed. She wanted some new boundaries, a new set of rules to follow.

It wasn't easy. It took some effort and courage. At first, her kids made it difficult for her. They tried to make her feel guilty, as if something was wrong with her. Just as many do when forced to accept new boundaries, they acted hurt and rejected. Because of her previous pattern of behavior, they felt that they were entitled to her time. Rather than being grateful for all she had done and was continuing to do, they felt ripped off. In reality, it was they—not her—who were being selfish. But she persevered, and it worked. She discovered that she could have it all—time for herself and time with her grandkids. And because she approached her new boundaries with loving kindness and honesty, her kids learned to accept, even honor them.

From time to time, couples need to set new boundaries, as well. Richard has always desired time to be alone. When our kids were very little, however, it was difficult for him to do so. As the kids have grown, he has been able to renegotiate his boundaries to include a little more time for himself. He has negotiated this with the kids and with me, and it's fine. He spends plenty of time with us—and has time left over for himself. If you were to ask him, he would tell you that renegotiating his personal boundaries has played a large role in his own personal happiness. I'm a bit that way, too. I enjoy going a few places by myself or with friends. I've set a boundary saying, "I need this for myself." Richard is very respectful of this need, and the kids are learning to be, as well.

I met a woman who said her husband freaked when she said she was no longer willing to do 100 percent of the housework. His response was, "You never used to mind." Give me a break! Can you see how important it would be for her to renegotiate?

The problem is, if you don't have the courage to say, "This is what I need," you're never going to get it! It's unrealistic that your spouse, children, or boyfriend is going to be able to read your mind, and even if they could, it's doubtful that they would be willing to set your boundaries for you. No way! If you've changed in some way and need to set new boundaries, whatever they might be, it's up to you.

This is an important topic that deserves some thoughtful reflection. This can be a tough strategy to implement, but in the end, it's well worth it. Good luck.

86

DON'T FIGHT FIRE WITH FIRE—
UNLESS IT'S A CONTROLLED BURN

When others lash out in anger at us or act in an aggressive or adversarial manner, it's tempting to fight back—to attack. So we argue, yell, and scream, or react defensively in some way. In a sense, we attempt to fight fire with fire. Yet, in the end, we usually wind up even more frustrated than before, and, more often than not, nothing is accomplished. Sometimes, all we do is fuel the fire and exacerbate the problem.

Everyone has conflict and is attacked from time to time. What seems to work best, however, is to fight your fires with what I like to call a "controlled burn." What I mean is that, while there is certainly a time and place for anger, it's ultimately how we deliver that anger—controlled or out of control—that will determine how our response is received. If we can remain relatively calm and collected, we will surely have a more powerful and meaningful impact.

I observed an extraordinary example of this strategy while shopping at a department store. A mother was with her teenage son, who became extremely angry with her because she wouldn't buy him something. He was acting spoiled and aggressive. Being a mother myself, I could imagine the thoughts that must have been going through her mind. Yet, the way she kept her composure was an example for us all. In a firm, no-nonsense, yet somehow compassionate way, the mother said to her son, "I know in my heart that you didn't mean to speak to me in that tone of voice, and I know that at some point today, you'll be offering me a sincere apology." I would have done anything to have it on video. I could have sold it at parenting classes around the world!

It's pure speculation, of course, but I can imagine what would have happened had the same person responded with loud, angry insults and put-downs to her son. Had she lectured him in a frustrated tone, rather than remained calm, it's almost certain that the tense moment would have escalated instead of gotten better. As it was, her "controlled burn" response made a difficult situation a little easier. The moment was put to rest and hurt feelings appeared to be minimized.

This strategy works wonders in almost any situation. The next time someone attempts to engage you in a blazing battle, give this strategy a try. Even if you're being taunted by someone, it should do the trick. Your inner confidence will appear unshakable, and that confidence will translate into your seeing most arguments and "fires" as relatively small stuff. Remember that when you fight fire with a controlled burn, you will be communicating far more effectively than when you're out of control. You'll leave any arguments you do have feeling much less stressed and more at peace, because you will have handled the problem from a true place of strength.

87

WHEN TRYING TO SIMPLIFY, THINK PREVENTION

So much has already been written on the relationship between simplifying and reduced stress. However, there is one aspect of simplifying that is often overlooked and, from my perspective, it may be the most important part of all—prevention.

Let's face it. Once something is in place—a source of stress, for example—it's often difficult, sometimes impossible to change it. Overscheduling our kids is a great example. They tell us they want to take ballet, soccer, gymnastics, T-ball, ceramics, you name it, so we sign them up for class after class. But by the time we've driven them around to all these extracurricular activities, they're exhausted and crabby, and so are we. (And often it's the Moms, as opposed to the Dads, who do most of the driving, for some reason.) Yet if we simply limited our children's after-school classes or sports to one extracurricular activity per season, we'd simplify our lives and cut down on our stress at the same time. It's pretty easy if you just think it out before agreeing to let them take every class they ask for.

The same logic applies to so many aspects of life. Richard and I have known people who serve on as many as four Boards of Directors of various companies and organizations. In addition to their normal work and family responsibilities, they are constantly rushing around to meetings. What seems odd is that these people always seem to wonder why they feel stressed and rushed! The problem was, they didn't prevent future stress by saying "no" to adding more responsibilities to their already too-full schedules.

Even if you love your pets dearly, you might want to say "no" to more until one of them passes away. With each new pet comes new trips to the vet, more messes to clean up, more food to buy, and one more creature who needs love, exercise, and your attention. Simply saying "no" to additional pets eliminates loads of future stress. Again, this has nothing to do with your love of four-footed friends. Rather, it's an awareness of the power of prevention.

If you have a career, there are only so many committees you can serve on and so many projects you can work on at once. If you have kids in school, there are only so many days you can work in their classes or so many fund-raisers you can participate in. By saying "no" to even more responsibilities, you are saying "yes" to yourself. Richard has always wanted to have a boat, and had decided to go ahead and get one. At the last minute, however, he postponed his decision. He started thinking that the fantasy may be better than the reality! He started thinking about cleaning, storing, maintaining a boat, and all the rest of it. I'm not sure what he'll decide in the end, but, being someone who really values simplicity, he seems pretty happy with his current postponement!

You can extend this same philosophy to simple things like magazine subscriptions and the like. Before you subscribe to one more, cancel your subscription to at least one other. Before making any more social dinner plans, make sure you have at least one weekend completely X'd out just for you; time when nothing is planned. Before adding anything to your life that you don't absolutely have to, try to anticipate what additional stress is going to come with it. If you're honest, it may be quite a bit.

88

SAY THE WORDS, "HEY, THAT'S A GREAT IDEA!" (AND THEN ACT ON IT)

If you're at all like me, you probably have some really great friends. And, other than the possible exception of your spouse, boyfriend, or parents, your friends know you better than anyone else. They know your strengths and weaknesses. They are aware of what makes you tick and what makes you fall apart. They can predict what is going to make you happy and what is going to drive you nuts!

So why is it then that when our friends—even our really, really good ones—offer us a suggestion or solution to a problem, we rarely, if ever take the advice? If you look at it neutrally, it's actually funny. Most of the time when advice is given, we respond in one of three ways. We either 1) tell our friend, "I've already tried that," which probably isn't entirely true; or 2) We immediately tell our friend the reason why "I can't do that," which is usually nothing more than a habitual response; or 3) We listen to the advice but never actually implement it. Instead, we continue doing things exactly as we have always done, which results in the exact same frustration.

I have an acquaintance from years back who has four adorable children, all boys. Her husband travels regularly on business, so the daily responsibility of raising the kids is pretty much in her hands. One of the problems is logistical; the kids are all over the map, age-wise. In addition to her infant, she has one who is nine, another twelve, and yet another who is fourteen. The kids are in all sorts of activities in all different parts of town. Unlike many other women, Geena is lucky enough to have plenty of money to get some outside help. But for whatever reasons, she won't do it.

A while ago I thought Geena was going to have a nervous breakdown. I know her well enough to know that it's extremely important for her to be really involved in her kids' lives. Yet, in reality, other than driving duty, she really wasn't that involved. By the time she would drop one child off somewhere, she was already late to another one's next activity, causing her ongoing stress and regret. She rarely had a chance to enjoy a single moment of any of her kids' sports or classes, as she was always scrambling to the next one.

She was also the "perfect" housekeeper, if there is such a thing. With no help whatsoever, she kept a beautiful house, made the lunches, helped with homework in the evenings, broke up the fights, and all the rest. Unbelievably, she even did most of the gardening! Let's face it, she was a martyr.

I can't tell you how many times I suggested that she at least see what it would be like to get some help. There were many things she could delegate, including some of the driving, cleaning, and yard work. There were also experienced yet affordable tutors available in her community who would love to help with at least part of the homework and who would probably do a better job than she could. I know for a fact that she could afford these luxuries, and I also know that she was quite comfortable allowing other moms and dads to drive her kids places, so the issue wasn't a fear of someone else behind the wheel. I've thought about it and, as crazy as it sounds, I'm convinced that the major reason she wouldn't take my advice (the same advice, by the way, that others have offered her, too) was that, very simply, it was being given by friends! Her automatic response and source of resistance seemed to be, "She couldn't possibly know how tough it is having four kids." And while she was right about that part of it, that didn't mean the advice wasn't sound and worth considering.

I've heard it said that the ultimate sign of maturity is when you can do something, even if your parents approve! Perhaps an accurate corollary could be, "A wise person is one who can take good advice—even if it happens to come from a friend or relative."

At first I thought Geena was really unique, but I've since realized that her resistance to taking advice from friends is actually a very typical response. To be honest, I realize that I, too, have some of the same resistance. For example, a friend might say, "Have you ever considered trying this or that with your kids—it really helps with the fighting." And, without even thinking about it, I'll catch myself responding with the old, "That's a good idea, but unfortunately it doesn't work with my kids." Then later, when I'm honest with myself, I'll realize that I've never even tried what my friend suggested.

I've finally realized that—not always, but certainly sometimes—my friends have some pretty darn good advice to offer. I've learned that taking it can be a shortcut to eliminating some pretty irritating sources of stress. My advice is this: The next time a friend or family member offers a suggestion—especially if you've shared a concern—take it to heart and give it some serious consideration. Who knows, it might be just the answer you're looking for.

89

DON'T TAKE IT ALL SO SERIOUSLY

This was an interesting strategy to think about because, on one hand, our lives are such a precious gift. Life is magical and important. Our concerns are legitimate. All of us have goals, plans, fears, and joys. From a certain perspective, we want to take it all very seriously, and believe me, I sometimes do. On the other hand, there's a way that we tend to take it all a bit too seriously and lose our lightheartedness along the way. Don't you agree?

My dad once shared with me a notion that our lives are a mere dash between the date of our birth and the date of our passing. In the scheme of things, we're here for a millisecond, a brief blip on the screen. Yet we act like every little thing is a giant emergency. Simply reminding myself of these obvious facts has been enormously helpful in my quest to keep things in better perspective, and to not take everything so incredibly seriously.

We lose perspective. Someone makes a mistake at work or at our kids' school, and it somehow turns into a federal case. We freak out (or at least overreact) when someone says the wrong thing, uses poor judgment, or looks at us wrong. We miss an appointment and we beat ourselves up emotionally. Never mind that we made the last three hundred appointments without a hitch. The phone has static, and we slam down the receiver. We forget that it's worked perfectly for the last two years, day in and day out. Our house is a bit messy and we act like we're entertaining the President. We lose our sense of humor because we turn so many things into a really big deal.

In a way, this strategy speaks to the essence of the "don't sweat" philosophy. It's the idea that in the hustle and bustle of daily living, with all the inherent hassles and responsibilities, it's easy to blow things way out of proportion. The good news is, by taking it even a little less seriously, we are able to bring back the joy, magic, and mystery to our daily lives.

Part of the solution involves being able to laugh at yourself, just a little. Try to see yourself (and everyone else too) as a character. Except for rare exceptions, we are all doing the very best we know how. The way I look at it, we have to learn to give ourselves a break—and others, too. This doesn't mean we lower our standards or put up with unethical or poor behavior, but it does mean we increase our perspective about things, especially "small stuff."

The next time you're in traffic, try this: Rather than feeling stressed and panicked, see if you can see the humor in so many people trying to get somewhere all at the same time. Imagine creatures from outer space looking down, wondering where everyone is going! Or, when you're in line at the post office or grocery store and the checker is talking to a coworker instead of speeding people through the line, see if you can turn it into a game. Just this once, try to see it from their perspective. See if you can think of a time you've felt like doing the very same thing (even if you didn't do it), when you were supposed to be responsible. Then, rather than giving the checker a lecture or sending them bad thoughts, smile at him or her when it's finally your turn. Practice making it less of a big deal. Amazingly, with a little practice, these things really won't seem so critical. In fact, you'll begin to notice that most people do an excellent job, most of the time. And even when they don't, you'll soon be home enjoying your dinner.

We were at an airport waiting to board a plane when the airline personnel announced a thirty-minute delay on a nonstop flight to Hawaii. Half the people started acting like the world was coming to an end! The reality, of course, was that all it meant was that they would have to wait thirty more minutes for their first Mai Tai in paradise! No one wants to be delayed, but then again, it's not that serious.

Aside from the truly painful parts of life, when looked at with a sense of humor, life really is pretty funny. And the more you try to see it that way, the less frustrating the hassles seem to be. If you learn to practice this strategy, you'll be smiling about things that used to drive you crazy!

90

FANCY YOUR FEMININITY

While being a woman can have its ups and downs, it helps to see that our femininity is cause for celebration. We are blessed with a myriad of choices of self-expression in terms of our appearance—from having a wide variety of clothes and shoes to choose from as well as our hair, makeup, and underwear.

There are many things I love about being female, and makeup and lingerie are in my top ten! While I find my husband's boxers quite sexy (on him), I also feel so lucky to be born female with my endless choices and selections. We have the best of both worlds; we can enjoy sexy lingerie as well as wear men's boxers.

Lingerie allows us to celebrate our womanhood every time we dress. I adore giving lingerie to my closest women friends. When you are feeling like you need a little perk, invest in some new bras and underwear, and toss those old ones goodbye.

On the days I look in the mirror and think, "Ugh, who is that looking back at me?", I feel grateful that I have the option of adding color to my eyes and cheeks. It's no wonder that some men like to use it, too! I feel like an artist every time I put on my face. I can wake up and look really blah, but after I put on my makeup, in just minutes, I feel like a totally different person. I'm not advocating caking the stuff on. In fact, most women look best when they use makeup lightly to enhance their natural beauty.

Feeling grateful about your femininity and enjoying your many choices of self-expression ought to help balance out your perspective on the days you feel it's a curse to be female.

91

KNOW YOUR HOT SPOTS

One of the reasons we walk around feeling frustrated and agitated with so many people around us is that we haven't identified our "hot spots"—our own patterns and Pavlovian responses to those buttons people seem to keep pushing. I mean, after all, if we could just fix everyone else, then we'd be happy. Right? Wrong!

One of the keys to being happier and handling life with more ease is to know your hot spots; those emotional triggers that leave you feeling vulnerable, frustrated, stressed, or agitated—those triggers that you consistently react to in a negative way.

When you know your hot spots, it's kind of like receiving a warning signal while you're on the tracks, so you don't get hit by a freight train. Knowing what tends to push your buttons allows you to take a step back; "see it coming," as it were; and make any necessary allowances so that you won't be bugged so much. In other words, instead of reacting as usual, you're able to say to yourself, "Oh, that again," or "Here it comes." It's a way of preparing yourself so that you don't take yourself—or that which bugs you—so terribly seriously.

One of my own hot spots is when one of my daughters reacts negatively to something I think they should be enjoying. For some reason, it tends to make me really frustrated, but, I'm happy to report, not as much as it used to. Ironically, while I was sitting down to write this particular strategy, one of my kids called me to tell me she "didn't want to go to her stupid soccer practice." Whereas I used to take this type of comment personally, I now understand that it's not personal at all; it's simply one of my hot spots. And knowing this about myself has been an enormous help.

I've learned that when the conversation begins to flow in that direction and I feel a twinge of frustration overtaking me—that "old familiar feeling"—I take a step back and say to myself, "I know I'm apt to be bugged by this. It's not worth it. I'm not going to allow it to get to me," or something along these lines. Amazingly, it takes the edge off, virtually every time. It affords me the necessary perspective to not take whatever it is, personally.

In my soccer example above, knowing my own tendency in this area allowed me to stay calm and compassionate, realizing that when I was that age, I wouldn't have wanted to be dragged to practice in 100-degree weather, either. For that matter, at my age now, I wouldn't want to practice anything in 100 degree weather. Plus, maybe she's tired, in a low mood, or having a bad day. Why in the world would I take her position personally? I'm not suggesting for a moment that I'm always able to stay calm and collected, but I am saying that by using this strategy, it's easier than before.

Everyone has their own hot spots. One of Richard's is that he reacts negatively when someone (a carpenter, for instance) starts a job he's being paid to do, but doesn't quite finish. It used to drive him nuts. I've noticed, however, that he's doing a lot better since he's recognized that it's one of his hot spots. He has been far more patient with others. The situation is, without question, a whole lot easier on his own nerves as well! He will probably always tend to be bugged by this issue, but it's a matter of degree. It seems that when you identify your hot spots, you're less likely to sweat the small stuff.

Whatever your hot spots happen to be, see if you can recognize them as such. You're going to be pleasantly surprised at how much less reactive you'll be to those things that used to make you crazy.

92

WALK THROUGH THE OPEN DOORS

If you're like most people, you have endured a time when you felt really muddled about the direction in which your life was going; which way you were going to navigate your ship, so to speak. I have certainly been through periods like these. Yet I have found that once I start pursuing a direction, whatever it may be, opportunities have a way of presenting themselves to me when I walk through the open doors.

Your attitude has everything to do with your ability to recognize when an open door has come your way. If your eyes are open to the possibilities in life, and you adopt a positive attitude (having faith that everything works out for the best in the end), the question will not be, "What am I going to do with my life?" It will be, "Which door do I walk through?"

Walking through the open doors, when combined with a certain degree of faith, is a truly Zen way of living. You forfeit the struggle by this leap of faith, believing that when you experience ease, it is a sign that you are on the right path. The opposite is also true. As you experience struggle, it can mean that perhaps you are off track. In these instances, follow your heart; your head will only confuse you.

It is our nature to be concerned with "making the right choice." When our goal is to make the right choice, we fill our heads up with all sorts of options and possibilities, so much so that we don't go anywhere. We get stuck right where we are. There are generally many paths which lead you to the same destination. While you may knock at a few that are closed, avoid beating down the doors that appear bolted. You can spend your precious energy beating down closed doors, or you can choose the doors that open when you knock.

As you continue on your journey, you will still face new challenges and choices. But as long as you keep choosing a path that seems to require the right amount of effort, you'll know you are walking through the open doors. However, when you are putting out great efforts and nothing seems to be happening, or you are not getting the desired result, it is a sign for you to move in a different direction. Chances are, when you have a strong, intuitive feeling or a passionate interest, you'll find some doors open along that path. If you choose the path of least resistance, the end result will probably be what you desired. The difference is in how much you struggle along the way.

Think in terms of walking through the open doors, and you will be surprised at the ease it brings to your daily choices.

93

OWN YOUR EMOTIONS

There's no question that one of the keys to a happy, fulfilled, and contented life is to make the decision, once and for all, to stop blaming others and outer circumstances for your emotions. This isn't to say that your emotions are wrong, stupid, inappropriate, or bad—only that they are yours.

Easier said than done, of course, but important, nevertheless. After all, most of us have the need, at least some of the time, to think about, obsess, complain, and commiserate over our perceived problems: the place in which we live, our career, husband or boyfriend, a person who grates on our nerves, the weather, the school our children attend, our neighbors, financial hardships, bad breaks, or whatever.

There's a tremendous difference, however, between complaining about any aspect of our lives and thinking it really is "life" that's getting us down, versus doing the same complaining, yet knowing deep down that it's really ourselves, our own thinking, that is creating our uneasy feelings. Let me share a simple example.

I was at a resort for a family vacation last winter when I overheard someone say, "This snow is driving me nuts." Yet clearly, the snow itself couldn't have been the culprit! There were thousands of people at the resort we were visiting, and almost everyone, with the exception of one overtired two-year-old, seemed to enjoy every second! Had the snow been causing people to go nuts, craziness would have abounded. The only possible explanation could have been this person's own thinking. Something inside of her was convincing her that the snow was bad: It was her own perception.

Because she blamed the snow for her unhappiness, she was doomed to have a negative experience. It was out of her hands; she couldn't be happy until a break in the weather allowed her that privilege. Had she been able to say, "Gee, I'm allowing my thoughts to get the best of me here. I'd better change my attitude or move to a lower elevation," she would have prepared for a change of heart. Notice that I'm not saying she had to pretend to like the snow in order to experience peace. All she had to do was stop *blaming* the snow.

The same principle exists in other matters. It's okay to be mad at your boss, but your boss can't control your thoughts—nor is she responsible for them. It's the same with regard to your neighbors, your kids, or your husband. Everyone can do irritating things, but there's a middleman between the "stuff" and people of your life, and the way you feel. That middleman is your own thinking, and owning this is an incredibly freeing insight.

I was talking to a parent at a soccer game who said, "My next-door neighbor is making me crazy." I could sense the pressure and stress that this person really did feel. Again, I'm sure you can empathize because we all have neighbors, and some are better than others. But to give your neighbor or anyone that much power over the way you feel is, in my book, a prescription for unhappiness.

Your emotions belong to you. Your happiness, depression, joy, sorrow, anger, and ease all are yours! Like it or not, and for better or worse, you carry them around with you, and you alone have the power to change them. But in order to change them or let go of them, you must first own them and admit they are yours.

I hope you'll reflect on this strategy and make an attempt to put it into practice in your life. The slightest shift in this direction can bring a sense of empowerment, confidence, and joy to your world.

94

REMIND YOURSELF WHAT IT
MEANS TO BE A HUMAN "BEING"

I sometimes wonder what Martians would think if they were able to look down and observe us. I'll bet they might be confused as to why we call ourselves "human beings" when our actions suggest we are really more like "human doings."

"Beingness," after all, is the state in which you are ever-present in whatever activity you are engaged in; i.e., absorbed in what you are currently doing. It suggests that this moment, not the next one (or the last one), is the most important moment in which to immerse yourself. Most of us, however, are so busy doing things, regretting other things, rushing around, and planning for other moments, that it sometimes seems as if we lose sight of the moment we are really in—this one.

Many people have heard the saying, "Life is what's happening while we're busy making other plans." Sadly, this is often the case. We become so preoccupied with what's going to happen, or what has already happened, that we lose sight of what is actually happening.

It's no coincidence that this frenetic pace in which we live is actually encouraging our spirits to starve and dry up. After all, it's taking more and more stimuli to satisfy us. Far from being easily satisfied, many of us are stimulus junkies, addicted to "what's next." Rather than being touched by life and its simple pleasures and beauty, we are consumed by our "to do" lists. We're too busy to be fully engaged in what we are doing because we're already planning the next activity. We say we want more time; yet, even when something is canceled, we usually find a way to fill it up with another activity. Then we complain again about having no time. The truth is, we're addicted to having no time because we don't know what to do with it once we get some.

We live in a technologically advanced society where even our most human experiences are often reduced to impersonal cyber-reality; where communicating with someone requires a modem. While the Internet is a remarkable tool for bringing information to your fingertips, there are many appalling uses with which people elect to engage their minds. When used improperly, it provides nothing more than an escapist's best solution for not "being" here now.

The best solution seems to be reacquainting yourself with your own "beingness"—that quiet part of yourself that exists independent of your busyness, goals, and responsibilities. This is the part of you that feels satisfied simply because it exists—rather than because it is accomplishing yet another task.

The way to go about reacquainting yourself with this wise and comfortable part of your consciousness is to experiment with doing nothing! That's right—nothing. As impossible as this may seem, the rewards are rich. Don't worry, I'm not talking about sitting around for hours. You can start with a minute or two, and work your way up. There is something magical about sitting or lying down and just being quiet, allowing your mind to clear and settle. In a way, our minds are like those snow globes that kids love. As we sit quietly, doing nothing, our minds have a chance to settle, calm down, rest, and become re-inspired. Without the chatter of our busy minds, our deeper intelligence has a chance to present itself. Instead of "us" doing the thinking, it's almost as if the thinking is done "for" us, from somewhere within.

As you practice, you'll find yourself much more comfortable with not filling every spare moment of your time with even more activity. This, in turn, will help you calm down your schedule and your life.

As you quiet down, you may find yourself reflecting on the miracle that you are alive and breathing. At around the age of three, both of our daughters exclaimed in astonishment, "Isn't it weird that we are alive?" It's that kind of inquisitive charm and astonishment that many of us have lost in our adult busyness of doing. But it's that same childlike enthusiasm that we can get back by simply becoming more aware of our beingness. Why not give it a try today? Your life can feel calmer and more peaceful than you ever imagined.

95

FIND YOUR COMPASSION CORNER

I view compassion as the ability to understand another's grief, pain, or hardship. It's about seeing life through the eyes of a homeless person or an emaciated Third World child. It is a genuine attempt to "put yourself in someone else's shoes," spending even a fraction of your time in the contemplation of the plight of a fellow human being, or a tortured animal, or a rain forest about to become extinct.

Deep inside ourselves, we all have our own compassion corner; the place in our heart where our compassion moves us so greatly that we feel we have no option but to give of ourselves in some way, however small. Mother Teresa said, "We cannot do great things on this Earth. We can only do small things with great love." As was so often true, she was right. But then again, there are so many "small" things we can do with great love. We can give our time, our love, ideas, support, money, expertise, or simply our heartfelt, nonjudgmental, loving thoughts.

Compassion is powerful on two fronts. Most obvious, of course, is that it encourages us to be a part of the solution; to do our part, whatever that may be; to be of service; to make the world a slightly better place. The gift of ten dollars a month may not seem like that much to you or me, but it can be the difference between life and death for someone else. Or, if money is tight, or if it's more your preference, volunteering your time, even a few hours a month, can make an enormous difference to someone in need or to an organization who needs loving help. Our daughter Kenna once said with excitement to Richard, "Daddy, if I pick up ten pieces of litter a day, that's 3,650 pieces of litter every year!" And she has followed through with her plan. If everyone did that, there would be very little litter to look at!

In addition to the service aspect of compassion, however, is the more personal aspect. The simple truth is, compassion and inner peace go hand-in-hand. When your heart is filled with compassion, it's almost impossible to be overly stressed or unhappy. Compassion is a feeling of warmth that soothes the soul. It's like a blanket of protection from any harmful effects of too much competition, stress, greed, anger, or ambition. It's an inner balancing mechanism that enables you to be on the one hand responsible, successful, and motivated; while on the other hand, relaxed, wise, generous, thoughtful, and calm. Compassion is so powerful that even if your only goal was to help yourself, it would still be worth it.

Compassion is something that grows with practice. The more attention you give to your "compassion corner," the healthier and more developed it will become. The key is to spend a little time each day reflecting on this critical aspect of humanity. In the beginning, setting aside even two or three minutes can make a world of difference. Sit quietly and reflect on how you can be of service. The rest will take care of itself. Clear your mind of your daily responsibilities, plans, and goals and simply allow your compassionate heart to send you ideas. Maybe you'll think of an organization you can help, or perhaps you'll think of a way to be a little kinder to the people you know.

Along those lines, it's also important to extend our compassionate heart into our daily lives. Can we be more patient with our family, friends, and coworkers when they make mistakes? Can we "let it go" when someone zips in front of us in traffic? Can we make allowances for the fact that all people have bad or "off" days? Can we remember to give our waitress a break when the service isn't perfect, or the ticket agent when the line seems to be moving too slowly? Can we smile at our grumpy neighbor even though he "doesn't deserve it," or listen to a friend or lover gripe, even though we're not in a great mood ourselves? These and thousands of other examples like them are the ways we can become more compassionate in our daily lives.

It's impossible to quantify, but I'd guess that if each of us would become even 10 percent more compassionate, we'd eliminate many of the ongoing problems in our world. Plus, we'd all be a lot happier, too! I hope you'll join me in my goal of making my own compassion corner just a little bigger and more visible. Let's each of us try to carve out a corner of our budget, our time, our thoughts, and our actions to create a beautiful collective corner in our hearts—our compassion corner.

96

REMEMBER THAT A LOW MOOD IS ONLY TEMPORARY

Moods don't matter much unless, of course, you're feeling low. When was the last time you pondered what was wrong with your life when you were feeling great? I'll bet never. If you're like most people, when you're high and on top of the world, your mood is as invisible to you as the wind.

So, what happens to us when we are low? When you're low, everything looks dramatically different—your job, relationships, family life, finances, problems, and everything else. A low mood has such a powerful influence over your perception of life that even your past can appear different. The reality, of course, is that it's not your life that changes from moment to moment; it's your mood.

An old saying comes to mind: "What goes up, must come down." Moods are no different from climbing a hill; at the top of every hill is a slope going down on the other side. Our minds cannot always remain "high" because we would not find balance otherwise.

It's helpful to remember that, whatever form it takes, feeling low is usually just that: feeling low. It's only when you entertain those feelings, make something of them, give them too much significance, or overanalyze them, that they take over and dominate your perceptions of life. It's a common fear, and incredibly scary, to think that when you're low, you will always remain that way. You'll notice, however, that if you can simply recognize that low moods are only temporary, and not make too much of them, you will soon be on the upswing to a better frame of mind.

There are times in life where we are confronted with real problems and issues that require our attention. Fortunately, however, most of life is filled with "small stuff" kinds of issues. These are the ones to learn how to acknowledge, but not give credence to. The time to tackle the real issues and problems is not when you're low, but when you are feeling capable. If, however, you must deal with a problem or situation when you're low—fires to put out at work, a personal conflict, some sort of bad news—understand that your judgment will probably be a bit skewed at that time. Exercise some mental caution. Question your judgment, and make allowances for the fact that you're low. Keep in mind that if the problem really does need your attention, it will still be there when your mood rises. When you're feeling better, your wisdom and common sense will be back. The same problems will look and feel dramatically different.

Let me give you a personal example. Just the other day, an issue came up at my daughters' school that was causing growing tension among the parents and administration. Due to a conflict among the staff, one of the best teachers was considering leaving our school. The parents—I among them—decided the best thing to do would be to write a letter on the teacher's behalf. As I sat down to reread my letter, I realized that my mood was not only low, but red-hot with anger. Even though I signed the letter with the intention of mailing it, I decided that there was no emergency and I should wait until after the weekend to see how I would feel about it. Sure enough, as my mood lifted, I felt that the letter was too harsh and needed to be softened.

Imagine, for a moment, that you have a "mood ring." The purpose of the ring is to remind you when you're feeling low. When it flashes bright red, it alerts you that it's time to take your thoughts and feelings a little bit less seriously. It tells you that now, more than at other times, you're going to be tempted to feel defensive, reactive, and judgmental. Your life is going to seem harder and more stressful than it probably is. You'll feel a sense of urgency, the need to try to "figure out" your life or solve your problems.

Despite the compelling urge to react to your low mood, it's your job to recognize that now is not the best time to attempt to sort things out. Far wiser to simply wait for the mood to pass, which it will do, on its own, if you simply let it be.

Of course, we don't have a flashing mood ring! We do, however, have an even more reliable tool at our disposal—our feelings. Our feelings tell us with pinpoint accuracy what our current state of mind is. All we have to do is tune in and pay attention to how we're feeling. When you're feeling low, that is your warning that your thinking is off. If you don't make too much of it, chances are, you'll be back up again very soon.

97

CLIMB YOUR MOUNTAINS ONE
STEP AT A TIME

I recently had the wonderful experience of spending some time with my dearest friend, Lisa, at her home in Italy. We looked forward to hiking up the mountain paths, which reveal spectacular vistas of lake, mountains, and old Italian villages.

When you look at a mountain, it's clear to see why they have long been a metaphor for life's challenges. As you stand at the bottom of the mountain, seeing it all at once, planning to climb it can seem like an overwhelming challenge. You immediately take it in, sizing it up, thinking self-doubting thoughts like: *That is going to be a tough climb. Boy, am I going to be tired. I don't know if I can make it.* But after the initial hesitation, you decide to go ahead, and one foot goes in front of the other while you pace yourself one step at a time.

As you bring your attention to your feet, you focus only on what's in front of you. You enjoy the climb and derive satisfaction from the experience by keeping your attention here, each step, each moment. If you focus on how far you have to go until the top, you become fatigued from the mere contemplation of it, thereby risking your ability to complete the climb. If you sneak a look down, you may become frightened at how far you have come, or you may feel exhausted. So, walking becomes a sort of meditation. As long as your thoughts don't muddle you, before you know it, you're at the top—and you did it one small step at a time.

We are all certain to experience challenges in our lifetimes. The mystery for each of us is which ones will be ours. Dealing with our challenges on a daily basis is no different from climbing a mountain one step at a time. You can handle any situation that appears to be an obstacle if you take it one step at a time, keeping your attention here, now. If you attempt to take in the whole problem at once, you risk not making it to the finish line. Don't contemplate the future; don't dwell on the past. During challenging times, we need all our resources available to us, and our thinking gets cloudy and unclear if we wander to past or future concerns. Challenges are far less overwhelming if you solve them in the moment with baby steps.

Your personal mountain may come to you by choice in a specific goal you set for yourself, or it may be that you are overcoming an addiction or facing news of illness. Remember that the journey of a thousand miles begins with a single step. Whatever the challenge, you will be able to face it, one step at a time.

98

DEFINE YOUR SMALL STUFF

It's really helpful, when trying to learn to stop sweating the small stuff, to define what you mean by "small." Then, when you're sweating about something, you'll have a reference point, a way to remind yourself to keep things in perspective.

Perhaps the easiest way to discover what is truly small is to think, for a minute, about what is big. We can all relate to the big stuff—serious illness, death, a drug problem, hunger, child abuse, a family emergency, bankruptcy, or the sudden loss of a job. Few would argue against the fact that things of this nature, and other serious stuff, are truly big.

When you think about it, however, this pretty much means that most everything else falls into the "small stuff" category. Obviously, neither Richard nor I consider it small when someone breaks into your home or steals your car. On the other hand, it's not quite the federal case we sometimes make it out to be when someone cuts us off in traffic, fails to return a phone call, or when our waist size is an inch more than we would like it to be. Indeed, before we define what we mean by small, many of us unconsciously define practically anything—the slightest glitch in our plans, the smallest irritation—as big stuff. And even if we don't define it as big, we certainly treat it as such!

While few of us probably love to do dishes, it's nevertheless helpful to remember how lucky we are to have them. The same applies to traffic. No one enjoys it, yet, all things considered, it's a luxury to have access to a car or other forms of transportation. When our children are complaining, it's a drag. On the other hand, what a blessing it is to have kids to love, even if they complain sometimes.

Unfortunately, no matter how much we believe it to be true, no amount of this gratitude "logic" alone will prevent us from sweating the small stuff. It is, however, a great place to start. Indeed, the first step is to begin to define things as small rather than big. Then, as you reinforce your healthier outlook, more and more things will appear, in your eyes, as small stuff.

Obviously, if I consider it an absolute emergency when the waiter brings me the wrong order, the line in the grocery store is moving too slowly, or Richard shows up fifteen minutes late, it's going to be difficult to be nonreactive. The only time I can possibly be happy, given these near impossible standards, is when life and all the people in it are treating me perfectly. Let's see, that happened once, about twenty years ago!

On the other hand, if I define these things—and the thousands of other potential sources of daily irritation—as small, then I've got a fighting chance to keep my cool.

The more things we define as small, the better off we'll be. As we get used to letting things go rather than clenching our fists and feeling frustrated, we will feel lighter and more peaceful. Not only will we feel more relaxed, but those around us will feel more at ease, as well. This will translate into better relationships, easier communication, and an overall enhancement in the quality of our lives.

One idea is to keep a mental list of all the things you consider to be "big stuff." Then, as things come up and you lose your cool, remind yourself of this concept. If whatever you're upset about isn't on that list, remind yourself to take it in stride. Take a few deep breaths and move on. After all, life will never be perfect. Yet, when we define our small stuff, it gets a whole lot easier to keep things in perspective.

99

BE ABLE TO STAND ON YOUR OWN TWO FEET

Women have never before had such numerous opportunities to accomplish anything we choose. We are no longer considered the "weaker sex" in the workplace or the sports arena. In this new millennium, everything is at our fingertips; we have more equal financial opportunity than ever before, and for the first time (other than in wartime) women are often the main breadwinners in their households. On the other hand, we can choose to stay home to raise our children and manage our homes. Many women conquer it all, balancing both career and family.

Yet, with all the options available to us, there are still women who find themselves suddenly widowed or divorced, and who don't know the first thing about their financial situation because of their previous dependence on their partner. No matter what your circumstances, you must be prepared to stand on your own two feet, both emotionally as well as financially.

While it's important not to live in fear of calamity, you can take an assessment of your skills and current marketability, even if you have no intention of seeking employment at this time. Even though your marriage may be happy and your finances stable, things can change rather suddenly. What happens to you if something happens to your partner? Are your finances secure? Are you aware of all of your investments, as well as insurance policies? Knowing this information is no more than "tying your camel" for the just-in-case scenario. It's best to be prepared, especially if you encounter an unexpected tragedy. One of the worst things, as I see it, would be to lose your partner, and in addition to grieving, not know how to provide for your family or have a plan of action.

A friend of mine woke up one day—as she explains it—not really knowing when it happened, but realizing that she was married to a crack cocaine addict. They shared two beautiful children. Her husband of ten years, now an addict, had ruined their bank credit and lost their house. She knew that her only choice was to walk out and stand on her own two feet before he dragged her and their children into the pit of hell with him.

With little money in her savings and facing bankruptcy, she drove around in her van for days, looking for someone who'd believe that she could pay her rent. It had been years since she left her sales career, but fortunately, she had kept in touch with her clients, and immediately got a job in an upscale office.

Three years later, with zero help from her ex, she owns her own house, sends her kids to private school, and even takes her family to Hawaii on vacation every couple of years. Her strength and capability is a great example of being prepared. She loved her husband greatly and never planned on leaving him, but she knew that if she had to, she could stand on her own two feet—and so she did!

Have you analyzed your marketability lately? If you had to go back to work, what would you want to do? Do you plan to go back to school to further your education and expand your horizons after your children are grown? I'm not much for the five-year plan, but sometimes it's important to gradually move in a chosen direction, rather than finding yourself in a desperate predicament because you weren't prepared.

Part of being able to stand on your own two feet is keeping abreast of your finances. Even though in our household, Richard makes the majority of our financial decisions in terms of investments, insurance policies, and so forth, he always keeps me well-informed. I know where we keep our important documents and contact numbers in case of any emergency. We have discussed what I would need to do if anything happened to him.

Being able to stand on your own two feet emotionally means that you are happy not only because of the partner in your life, but because your life is full of challenges, rewards, and meaning. We must not look to another individual for our fulfillment; instead, we must look to ourselves. Being fulfilled is not something you can delegate. You must take charge of your own happiness and emotional well-being.

Being prepared to stand on your own two feet will take the stress out of wondering whether or not you could if you ever needed to. When everything is in order, it's a lot easier not to sweat it!

100

TREASURE THE JOURNEY

Ah . . . what a concept: Treasure the journey. Before your mind skips to the trials and tribulations that you may face today, or the fact that today your life might not be what you had expected or hoped for, take the time to repeat these words to yourself: Today, I will treasure the journey.

To "treasure" something means to hold it close to your heart. When we talk about treasuring the journey, what I mean is that we hold the gift of life itself with the highest regard; to make it an adventure marked by your personal path of discovery.

Richard often says in his lectures, "Life is a process, not a destination." It's not like you're going to "get somewhere" and all will be well. Instead, the joy is in the path itself. Your journey is the day-to-day, moment-to-moment process, and the attitude that you bring to that path has everything to do with what you will receive along the way. The question is this: Do you anticipate what life is going to be like someday, or do you live life as it unfolds right now? Your answer will determine whether your life is experienced as an adventure, or whether it's constantly on hold until further notice!

I'll admit that there are days when we wake up and it feels more like we will be trudging through a muddy trail, with poison oak on all sides, than skipping freely through a meadow of wildflowers with the wind in our hair. It's precisely on these heavier days that we must remember to treasure the journey.

It's helpful to remind ourselves that on every great vacation we've ever been on, at least one thing went wrong, yet we refused to let it ruin our good time. It's with this same spirit that we must embark upon each day as a new beginning that holds an adventure in the wings of each moment. (Some of which, admittedly, we'd rather not go through again.)

I was once sitting in a café in Berkeley in a reflective state of mind. I watched all the people walking by for several minutes. With each person's appearance screaming "individuality" as they do in Berkeley, I thought to myself how grand it is that there are as many different people as shapes and colors. I was acutely aware that each person who walked by had their unique story to tell, complete with a past, present, and future.

The culmination of our experiences completes our own unique biography; every person makes their mark in history with their own story to tell, and each day represents the turning of the page. From the time you wake until the time you go to sleep at night, you mark your journey in fleeting moments and passing days. As you make it your single-minded intention to treasure this journey you are on, you begin to feel great gratitude as well as great love. You see that life gives you all of what you need, and some of what you ask for. Every event has purpose and meaning, and you know that "the small stuff" doesn't really mean much at all. In fact, it's fretting and worrying and dwelling on the small stuff that keeps you from treasuring your experiences daily.

As women, we have the world at our fingertips, with everything within our reach for the first time in history. All we have to do is spread our wings, navigate our direction with some good common sense and a lot of heart and soul, and fly like the wind.

So, make it a habit to wake up each day with the intention to see life as an incredible adventure—a journey to be treasured. Life is a great gift; it is the treasure at the end of the rainbow. As you begin each day, keeping this in mind, you'll experience wonder and awe as you open yourself to bliss.

As I close, I'd like to thank you for reading this book and sharing this treasured part of my journey.

With heartfelt affection
in love and light,
Kris

AUTHOR'S NOTE

The author supports the Susan G. Komen Breast Cancer Foundation. Please send your donations to:

Susan G. Komen Breast Cancer Foundation
PO Box 650309
Dallas, TX 75265-0309

For more information, contact: www.komen.org

SUGGESTED READING LIST

Carlson, Richard. *Don't Sweat the Small Stuff For Teens*. Hyperion, 2000.

———. *Don't Sweat the Small Stuff in Love*. Hyperion, 1999.

———. *Don't Sweat the Small Stuff at Work*. Hyperion, 1998.

———. *Don't Sweat the Small Stuff with Your Family*. Hyperion, 1998.

———. *Don't Sweat the Small Stuff About Money*. Hyperion, 1997.

———. *Don't Sweat the Small Stuff . . . and It's All Small Stuff*. Hyperion, 1997.

———. *Slowing Down to the Speed of Life* (with Joseph Bailey). HarperSanFrancisco, 1998.

———. *Handbook for the Heart* (with Benjamin Shield). Little, Brown, 1995.

———. *Handbook for the Soul* (with Benjamin Shield). Little, Brown, 1994.

———. *Shortcut Through Therapy*. Plume, 1995.

———. *You Can Feel Good Again*. Plume, 1994.

———. *You Can Be Happy No Matter What*. New World Library, 1997.

Bach, Richard. *The Bridge Across Forever: A Love Story*. William Morrow & Co., 1984.

———. *Jonathan Livingston Seagull: A Story*. Avon, 1995.

Bailey, Joseph. *The Speed Trap: How to Avoid the Frenzy of the Fast Lane*. Harper San Francisco, 1999.

Beck, Charlotte Joko. *Everyday Zen: Love and Work*. Harper San Francisco, 1989.

Borstein, Sylvia. *It's Easier Than You Think: The Buddhist Way to Happiness*. Harper Collins, 1995.

Borysenko, Joan. *Minding the Body, Mending the Mind*. Bantam Doubleday Dell Publishing, 1993.

Breitman, Patti and Connie Hatch. *How to Say NO Without Feeling Guilty*. Broadway Books, 2000.

Chopra, Deepak. *Ageless Body Timeless Mind: The Quantum Alternative to Growing Old*. Three Rivers, 1998.

Dyer, Wayne. *Real Magic: Creating Miracles in Everyday Life*. Harper Paperbacks, 1993.

Eadie, Betty J. *Embraced by the Light*. Bantam Books, 1994.

Easwaran, Eknath. *Take Your Time: Finding Balance in a Hurried World*. Nilgiri Press, 1994.

Gawain, Shakti. *Creative Visualization*. New World Library, 1995.

Gibran, Kahlil. *The Prophet*. Alfred A. Knopf Publishing, 1923.

Gittleman, Ann Louise. *Super Nutrition for Women: A Food-Wise Guide for Health, Beauty, Energy, and Immunity*. Bantam Doubleday Dell Publishing, 1991.

Hahn, Thich Nhat. *The Miracle of Mindfulness: An Introduction to the Practice of Meditation*. Beacon Press, 1976.

Hay, Louise L. *You Can Heal Your Life*. Hay House, 1999.

Hesse, Herman. *Siddhartha*. Bantam Classic, 1982.

Jampolsky, M.D., Gerald. *Love Is Letting Go of Fear*. Celestial Arts, 1988.

Jampolsky, Ph.D., Lee L. *Smile for No Good Reason*. Hampton Roads Publishing Company, Inc., 2000.

Kabat-Zinn, Jon. *Wherever You Go, There You Are: Mindfulness Meditation in Everyday Life.* Hyperion, 1994.

Kornfield, Jack. *A Path With Heart: A Guide Through the Perils and Promises of Spiritual Life.* Bantam Books, 1993.

Moore, Thomas. *Care of the Soul: A Guide for Cultivating Depth and Sacredness in Everyday Life.* Harper Collins, 1992.

Moran, Victoria. *Creating a Charmed Life: Sensible, Spiritual Secrets Every Busy Woman Should Know.* Harper San Francisco, 1999.

————. *Lit from Within: Tending the Soul for Lifelong Beauty.* HarperSanFrancisco, 2001.

————. *Love Yourself Thin: The Revolutionary Spiritual Approach to Weight Loss.* New York: Signet, 1999.

————. *Shelter for the Spirit: How to Create Your Own Haven in a Hectic World.* New York: HarperCollins, 1998.

Northrup, Christiane. *Women's Bodies, Women's Wisdom: Creating Physical and Emotional Health and Healing.* Bantam Doubleday Dell Publishing, 1998.

Levine, Stephen. *A Gradual Awakening.* Anchor/Doubleday, 1989.

St. James, Elaine. *Simplify Your Life: 100 Ways to Slow Down and Enjoy the Things That Really Matter.* Hyperion, 1994.

————. *Living the Simple Life: A Guide to Scaling Down and Enjoying More.* Hyperion, 1996.

Shinn, Florence Scovel. *Your Word Is Your Wand.* Beekman Publishing, Inc., 1999.

————. *The Game of Life and How to Play It.* Beekman Publishing, Inc., 1999.

Weil, M.D., Andrew. *Spontaneous Healing: How to Discover and Enhance*

Your Body's Natural Ability to Maintain and Heal Itself. Ballantine Books, 1996.

Books on Yoga:

Instant Stretches for Stress Relief: Instant Energy and Relaxation with Easy to Follow Yoga Stretching Techniques. Mark Evans. Lorenz Books, 1996.

Yoga: Mastering the Basics. Sandra Anderson and Rolf Sovik. Himalayan Institute.

Yoga Mind & Body. Sivananda Yoga Vedanta Center. DK Living, 1998.

Richard Hittleman's Yoga: 28-Day Exercise Plan. Richard Hittleman. Workman Publishing, 1969.

Yoga Videotapes:

Yoga Alignment and Form: A Home Practice With John Friend. Spring, TX: Purple Pentacle Enterprises.

Yoganetics: A Breakthrough Fitness Program That Extends Yoga Into Motion. Shawnee Mission, KS: Wyatt Townley; www.yoganetics.com

Stress Relief Yoga for Beginners: Suzanne Deason. Healing Arts Publishing; Living Arts: 1 (800)-2-living.

Meditation Tapes:

The Celestine Meditations: A Guide to Meditating Based on the Celestine Prophecy. Salle Merrill-Redfield. 1995 Time Warner Audio Books: 9229 Sunset Blvd., Los Angeles, CA 90069.

Deep Relaxation with Ali Hammer: Guided Relaxation With Music. AlijsjYahoo.com

AND DON'T FORGET THE MEN...

If you found this book helpful, you'll want to let the men in your life know about **Don't Sweat the Small Stuff For Men**, Richard Carlson's soon-to-be bestseller in bookstores everywhere **September 5, 2001**.

From families and love to work and money, Richard Carlson has helped millions learn how not to sweat the small stuff. Now, with six bestselling titles under his belt and over 12 million copies in print, Richard Carlson is back again, and this time he is helping men learn how to de-stress in today's competitive world.

With numerous simple strategies and life lessons that blend humor, warmth, and uncommon wisdom, Carlson offers men sound advice on how to relax and live in a more productive and calm manner, such as:

- Be a Quitter
- Get Out of the Serious Mode
- Rid Yourself of a Busy Mind
- Grant Yourself One Hour
- See Stress as Non-Sexy

Read a chapter from *Don't Sweat the Small Stuff For Men* at dontsweat.com. The first 100 people to respond about the book get a free copy.